Summary of Dissertation submitted for M
the *Reverend Patrick Reginald Andrew Reid*

A THEOLOGY OF GAME SHOOTING

Game shooting has become big business. It earns considerable foreign currency and injects money into local rural communities. In the Hillside Parishes, here, the development of one shoot has been the biggest recent farming investment. Yet shooting is controversial in that many who do not participate abhor it, usually from ignorance and failure to appreciate the whole picture and pattern of shooting. It has its roots back in the earliest days when man hunted for meat and still plays out that instinct. I had a shot gun for my 11th birthday and shot my first grouse in Scotland at the age of 13. Now, as a sport and an industry, game shooting is very much part of the make-up of my parish. I, therefore, seek to look beyond the good, the bad and the ugly, which features comprise many sports today, to something beyond that is spiritual, supportive and searching.

Game shooting takes place on private property, thus the start point must be the rights of property and ownership. However, added to that there is the consideration of property as an expression of the personality. The same is true of shooting. Therefore in Chapter I we look at (i) Aristotle and the Old Testament, (ii) The Medieval Debate; and (iii) Theology and Stewardship.

Chapter 2 considers changes in farming (i) Responsibility and Private Ownership; (ii) The Economics of Plenty, followed by (iii) the Options for Farmers Today and therefore a particular look at (iv) Set-Aside or Diversification, and lastly a theology (v) of Set-Aside.

Chapter 3 looks at shooting as part of these changes (i) In the Community; (ii) Its Economics, and (iii) The Future.

Lastly there are the ethics of shooting, as we look at shooting as a sport (i), and the need to shoot (ii). Then there are our attitudes towards animals (iii) the respect of animals, and the part that has to play in conservation (iv) finishing with a look at theology and shooting (v). At the end of the day it is not so much why we do it but how we do it. If done with due consideration for the quarry, shooting can remain above criticism.

Recession and the ability to produce enough food has hit the farming industry. In the Hillside Parishes in North Yorkshire (75 sq miles between the A19 and the west edge of the North Yorks Moors from the A170 at Thirsk) with 12 villages, the major investment has been in shooting on one estate. This provides 3 keepers once more, as many as 15 years ago, when the shoot was a purely private family affair, besides injecting other income into the area. The returns on this pheasant crop are fairly quick and the investment is by a third party who has developed the shooting and pays the keepers, so the farmers are not held to ransom by the Banks on high interest payments. But where does it all fit in?

There has been an on-going debate about the ethics of shooting for the last eighteen months, notably in The Field, because the behaviour of some is "not cricket". Certainly some participants are greedy, and many ignorant, though much of the criticism raised against those who participate in shooting is largely through ignorance.

Shooting and hunting do ensure the survival of the fittest so wild stock is strong stock.

ACKNOWLEDGEMENTS

One of the penalties of having a retired Prof. of Theology as an honorary assistant is that it is not so easy to argue with him when it comes to further study. However advantages are there in having a ready consultant, not that Anthony Hanson shoots, and not that I have taken advantage of having his support by giving him my essays to write. However, despite glandular fever just before the onset two years ago, it has been helpful to my ministry to order further studies along the lines of what goes on in my parish. Therefore my thanks to the York Diocese for enabling me to do the T.U.I.S. course of my in-service training.

I would also like to thank the Dept. of Theology at Hull and its staff and students for their interest and support, particularly the Revd. Drs. Barry Thompson and Peter Sedgwick. The latter has my heartfelt thanks for his encouragement and patience with someone who would far sooner down a book and be up and about on the moors. My thanks, too, for the time that friends with estates, farms and shoots have given me, and to various keepers whom I have quizzed or badgered for details. I leave them nameless here and in the text, lest the anti-bloodsports protesters should invade their shoots and jeopardize their livelihoods, which is a sad reflection on our times. I therefore dedicate this project to that profession, to whom ramblers and others who do not shoot owe so much more, and wish them well for the future.

Nicola and the children, Poppy, Briony and Sorrel, have been patient and amazed, the latter not least because I set off to my "school" sometimes at the same time as they did. It was therefore fun to share on that level, along with Nicola if she came beating occasionally. This would not be complete without mention of the late Bunbury who was a noble companion and whose obituary I put in this year's Regimental Magazine "The Yeoman".

My thanks, too, to those churchwardens and friends with shooting who have asked me kindly as a guest on their shoots, so participation has remained at all levels whilst working out my thoughts on this subject.

Finally my heartfelt thanks to Mrs. Ina Mallen for her skill in reading my writing and typing up the scripts, and to her husband James for sustaining us both with a jar or two of Highland nectar. The latter gesture will be rewarded in this life rather than just the one to come!

University of Hull
Leake Vicarage
September 1990 Toddy Hoare

October 1996: I would like to add my heartfelt thanks to my sponsor for seeing this into print for a wider audience, and to one of my churchwardens for the loan of his dog Binka to work on the moors on the odd shooting day. My thanks and God bless all true sportsmen.

Toddy Hoare

CONTENTS

A THEOLOGY OF GAME SHOOTING

INTRODUCTION

"Nisus; he was Hyrtacus' son and had come from the hunting grounds of Ida to follow Aeneus. A lightning shot with arrow or javelin". Virgil, Aeneid - Book 9 line 175.

As English society is no longer land based it is harder for people to understand and accept the realities of nature. They no longer see God's creation right on their very doorsteps. The domestic pet gives few clues unless from a working strain and used as such. Granted the warmth of towns may ensure the survival of more small birds than before and the attraction of the domestic dustbin may be such that whereas the almost extinct red kite in Elizabethan times was as common as the present pigeon on Nelson's column so is now the feral fox in urban areas. At the end of a day's shooting there is something for the table and therefore a product.

The question must be asked at what price to nature and at what cost to God's creation? Is it stewardship or slaughter or sport? Shooting yesterday may have been responsible for the shape of the landscape as we see it today but now so many seek to make money out of it, what is the effect?

In the past such sport has mainly been the prerogative of the countryman and those who come to work their dogs. Now the gun will reside as readily in the town as in the village and is not confined to the owners of the large country estates and private farms. An useful background is the parish and village life for it is here that the participants of the country sports meet and jostle for the space and their respective quarries.

If we look at Jesus' teaching and the environment or system that existed and on which he based his illustrations we will see that little has changed when it comes to the ownership of the land and what that owner can do with it. Whether he owns it outright or by whatever means, or has bought it or rents it on a long term covenant he has the responsibility for it: The vineyard owner, Matt. 20,1-16 or 22,33-end. The rich man, Luke 16,1-15. Man going abroad Matt.25,14-30. Little has changed. The owner, the capitalist who has to spend on it or rent it to get anything out of it, is free to do with his own as he pleases. To a certain extent that is still true today. Economics, market trends, wars or Government policies during wartime until changed, all cause a different approach for each generation and influence change but at the end of the day the farmer is an entrepreneur out to make a living from his capital - his farm and probably his inheritance - and enjoy it. What right has he to be there and to shoot over it or charge others for the pleasure?

CHAPTER 1

The Rights of Property

"It is just as important for our future now to wring the last ounce of food from our acres year by year as it was in the dark days of war".
W.S. Churchill." P.M. 1953.

(1) Aristotle and the Old Testament on Property

As a general law occupation has proved to be nine tenths of possession of any property. Fear or respect of the owners has ensured his possession in his absence. Some societies were dependant on slave labour running things and doing the work so the landlord was an absolute owner in that respect. It could be argued that today the pay packet is the owner of the person and commands virtual slave labour thus making the person employed akin to property of the firm with company posts, guarantees and pensions. In Japan the person is encouraged to regard the business as his extended family, which suggests not only better welfare on the one hand, but a greater control over the rest of the employee's life as well. Yet back within our own shores it can be argued that tied cottages on the land have offered both security and a reason for staying put in bygone years to those who worked the land. What has often remained unsaid is that also that status quo has been willingly accepted for the most part because the labourer felt he belonged to more of a family unit. Within the community he was unlikely to starve, there were holiday festivities and his basic needs were met. As model estates *1 sprang up in the C18th & C19th and church schools were provided the lot of his family improved, although it was a foolish squire who did not regard the welfare of his workforce.

The whole concept of the pyramid of ownerships is rooted in the way man has organised his society, from the time he has had to live together with his neighbours. Aristotle *2 was moved to ponder on

Plato's ideal of a commonwealth that had a very special and limited system of communal living for the ruling elite. Aristotle posed a question much voiced since and no doubt not new to him that "Those who labour little and consume much will always be open to criticism by those who labour much and have little to consume". *3 Thus should citizens of the perfect state have their possessions in common or not? How perfect the state is and how well it runs or how much it depends on ownership to take an interest and make the decisions, whether right or wrong in the longrun, can only be answered by experience. It is an ongoing question and one generation will always be analysing its own and previous experiences. Here is the stuff of application of history.

Aristotle saw the distinction between master and slave, ruler and ruled, as a natural one and similarly there is an order in nature and creation whereby plants exist for animals and animals exist or man, (Politics) However he reverses his argument in Metaphysics when considering how the nature of the whole possesses the good, for soldiers and the general are both good, as is the household of free men and slaves where all make a contribution. *4 If alive today perhaps he would remark that where people band together to ensure the common welfare of, say, shooting, there good is in evidence.

Whether in Greek city states or on the horizons of the Roman empire land was held, owned, cultivated and used. Soldiers on retirement would obtain land and thus a livelihood. The Romans were most legalistic in their attitudes: Cicero stated that "all men by the law of nature are equal". The Christian church would amend that to "All men in the sight of God are equal". There may be grounds for an entitlement to land but does everyone want it and can they all manage it? Those without a trade could earn their living working for another on his land. It is against this that the Jewish concept of a year of Jubilee *5 "sabbath of sabbath years" *6 is aimed. A man may lose his all but he is not to be enslaved forever. His property is his own and his family's, held in trust from God and therefore not to be forfeited. It has to do with sanctity of ownership and provision for the future but it also involves forgiveness and the development of the same as the law of love.

Rowland *7 makes the point that central to the covenant was the promise of land. The theme of Deuteronomy is the covenant between an obedient people and a God who gives his people land. The Exile prompted Jeremiah to comment on the relationship of God's promise and God's people, (chs 24,29,32). The Baptism of John can be seen as a development of the spiritual where by repenting (turning again) and coming up out of the water of baptism in the River Jordan the individual re-entered the promised land but with no extra material benefits than those already owned. In Jesus' teaching the promised land becomes the Kingdom which is a present reality depending on the spiritual response of the individual. Thus to "own the world" takes on a very different meaning!

Commentators *8 on the rights of property deduce that in the O.T. the prime concern of the Lord God in the use of land is the well being of all his people. Had the Israelites been happier in Egypt and better treated there they would have stayed. Even in the wilderness experience Egypt seemed preferable by contrast! *9 Anything less than the commonwealth is identified as theft of the property from God by whoever, whether monarch or landlord. Land ultimately reverted to the original owners and God is the overlord to whom Israel owed feudal service. *10 David gave thanks and the offering "Thine O Lord is the greatness, the power,..." *11 uses words on which the modern offertory prayer is based. In the light of relationships of man to property Justice is seen in a different perspective, for through the monarch it is about ensuring a form of self support. Thus God's grace was not so much a channel of his providence as the means of enabling the common lot through co-operation within the community. *12 Much of the message of the prophets is their preaching against the abuse of welfare .*13 God's property is given to us on trust and like the parable of the talents we dig and bury it at our own peril. *14

The real distraction from God is Mammon, usually associated with money but equally recognisable as currency. In the latter form it is easier to envisage Mammon subject to God. In the end perhaps mammon is most identifiable with the "time of trial" mentioned in the Lord's prayer. Is man faithful or does he have sticky fingers? How well man stewards his property and with what options is a question best answered later on. Currency can also be extended to charity. Money is not a vehicle for obtaining heavenly credit by just giving it away and disposing of the land or property that was its capital source but rather it is there as a challenge to use it as a means of providing for others. *15 It too can be hallowed. Thus stewardship has a wide range of obligations pointing to a commonwealth.

Possession is nine tenths of the law, but for a person to be too assertive "That is mine" like Tom Tiddler, is devaluing. He is an unworthy, even undeserving owner. If that person recognises a spirituality about ownership or the authority of God, according to his stance, and can say "I am God's" then he or she may not be a better owner but they are more conscientious. *16 The tradition is strong that property is a trust. Thus the landlord has to make his presence and his values felt against those with lesser reasonable values. Land is an extension of the personality as much as an exercise of that trust. Hegel argues that personality needs property for full development. As we cannot all have access to property are we less people?

The artist and craftsman may lack land but their work and manufactures are products of their self expression as is, to a lesser extent, the decor the wife makes in a home. These and many others who labour are not lesser people. However Hegel *17 argues that life's meaning is found in the concrete history of the human race thus reviewing mankind as a whole. His logic claimed to do for the whole of human knowledge what Aristotle's logic accomplished for the demonstrative reason, being a logic not of mere being but of becoming, through being, essence and notion.

We are accountable to God "To whom much is given, much is expected". Property may actually be a burden, rather than a challenge or a blessing, or an opportunity of personal development and expression. That people have to find alternatives to make their estates or farms pay is also a mixed blessing and some do go over the top. *18 Their expression through their property may not put them in their best light. Whilst some encourage children to learn from nature others give themselves away in their treatment of nature! One of the most popular alternatives at the Lightwater Valley Leisure farm is the intensive pig unit.

(ii) The Medieval Debate

"Thou hast given him dominion over the works of thy hands; and hast put all things under his feet, all sheep and oxen, and also the beasts of the field, the birds of the air, and the fish of the sea".

Psalm 8 vv 6-8

Albertus Magnus, like Alexander of Hales, in the middle ages made response to Aristotle, "asserting that communal ownership was natural in a state of innocence but private property was the natural way of providing for a man's family and the poor in a state of sin". *19 Thus in times of crisis, as already mentioned, the property of all becomes common. On the other hand in his day there were not so many owners and "Dieu et Mon Droit" was more applicable. St Thomas Aquinas also weighed up natural laws of possession. "Man to be naked is natural law because nature did not provide clothes. Art invented them. Thus while to hold things in common was a natural law, the distinctions of possessions and slavery were devised by human reason for the benefit of human life". John of Paris remarked "Acquisition of external goods by laymen through their own efforts gives them true possession and no one else has dominion over it" but this was also at a time when the Papacy was at its temporal height and its office holders tended to be somewhat hereditary and rather acquisitive!

However the debate on property goes deeper and again Thomas Aquinas takes up the challenge. *20 St Augustine had said "No" to the question "Whether in a state of innocence man would have been master over man?" Thomas said "Yes" quoting Aristotle as saying "Man is naturally a social being". Thus the ruler is bound by natural law to maintain the general system of private ownership and direct it for the common good.

The turning point in land ownership and rights was the Statute of Merton in 1236.*21 It was an attempt to limit disputes over the enclosure of common land. It empowered lords to enclose manorial waste provided they left sufficient pasture for their free tenants. Thus the rights of the latter became enshrined in national law. It marked a significant decline in the independence of villeins, as they received no compensation in future for the loss of customary rights. For the first time something wider than customary rights was attempted on a national scale.

In 1066 there were 60 Benedictine foundations owning 15% of land of England and having to provide some Knights with land to fulfil their military obligations. By 1400 there were 700 abbeys and monasteries holding nearly 25% of the land, much of which was donated since the 12th Century although sometimes with strings attached like hospitality, the boarding of hounds, and the right to nominate candidates for vacancies. However monasteries were not subject to dynastic accidents, failures of bloodline or confiscation if their politics differed, so they grew the whole time despite occasional bad management by an abbot more spiritual than temporal. Sometimes they absorbed the properties of heiresses too. Grants of land to religious orders were curtailed by the Statute of Mortmain 1279 and the Statute of Westminster 1285 whereby heirs of misused land given to monasteries could claim it back. Yet such stability of land ownership in the long term enabled the monasteries to carry out improvements and other schemes of capital intensive farming like drainage projects in the Fens. The Cistercians were successful with sheep and wool on remoter marginal land. Thus monasteries established patterns of land use and were able to impose innovations and even relocate settlements. Further revenue came from the pilgrim industry and by a strange coincidence relics were always discovered after disastrous fire! (Canterbury 1174, Glastonbury 1184). Little wonder that Henry VIII treated the monasteries as a useful bank just as his medieval predecessors had borrowed from the Jews to whom they gave banking licences to build and then threatened them death or baptism on the day of reckoning (Holocaust at Clifford's Tower, York C12th one such example). Even today where building stone was freely available elsewhere the ruins of the great monasteries, esp Rievaulx and Fountains etc testify how they dominated and influenced the landscape.

By Henry VIII's time the monasteries had become too landed. The principle of no ownership and property but a sense of owning the whole world, or equality as dictated by the exercise of ones talents, was sound: but wealth and power are accumulative and tempting to monarchs with a rumbling exchequer. They outgrew themselves and a revolution took place. History noted the nature of the final straw rather than the other factors.

In an essay on Possessions, Property and Human Nature, Canon Scott Holland, defends property owning. Firstly, Man is more careful with what is his. Secondly, Man is a better steward with continuity and order. Thirdly, Man is more content if secure and a peaceful state more likely. This was Thomas Aquinas' argument for property, inheritance and responsibility. Man is free to procure and to dispense and to possess property. Thus ownership is similar to individual possession of cottages in a row. Noise, smell, dangerous acts may upset the neighbours with good cause. Similarly how a man uses his property or land may cause offence and he may have to be answerable to others if the commonwealth is at stake. It is a debate open to the interests of others other than just a difference of opinion. The issues at stake may be legion, as a cross-section of the press and media may illustrate. Conservation, animal husbandry or cruelty may be more realistic points than personal preference for something like the pursuit of bloodsports.

Yet perhaps the attitudes we inherit were largely formed in the middle ages. What has passed for centuries as the Christian distrust of wealth is more likely rooted in the envy of it. Considering the ideal as copied from the practice of the early Christians "who sold property and held everything in common" *22 even communities or Kibbutzes came up against problems. When the parousia does not take place in the way initially envisaged there is reason not to hold things in common.

(iii) Theology and Stewardship

"The nation expects many things of farmers beyond food production. Not all of them can be provided by the market mechanism, so additional incentives are necessary .... the Countryside Commission suggests a new scheme is required which is directed towards multiple objectives, notably the environmental, recreational and social benefit which can be gained from farming." *23

The real question to be asked is "can a man do as he likes with his property?" The answer must be yes, so long as he does not infringe the privacy of others or their rights (bridle paths/access etc) or devalue what he tenants out. He has rights but he also has duties and there are limitations. Jesus' teaching draws very heavily on a status quo where there is ownership and wealth. Jesus' presentation of himself as the only son sent to claim the fruits of the vineyard by the owner from the tenants is a classic picture that time does not fade. Property is defended on a national scale by laws and the defence policy There are responsibilities to the public, be it only to warn of a bull in a field or similar. Most would feel they hold property in trust for the next generation *24 rather than from God but perhaps the church has too much opposition from other sources to get that message across. Government policies, subsidies, incentives, E.E.C. policies and controls, options for set aside all come into play as to how the property owner can set out to enjoy his ownership. As entrepreneur he is today in perhaps a similar boat to those making the first enclosures. Enclosures were not necessarily one man enveloping tracts of land behind his demesne wall but as much common action by a group to enclose land they had the use of in proportion to their respective rights. It's easier to grow your corn when your neighbours sheep only come on your land when you fallow it than having them trample it all year.

Naturally entrepreneurship in any shape has to take account of dominion over the beasts of the field and the birds of the air in one form or another. A man's swamping his estate with pheasants to exercise his shooting rights may mark time with the fashion of the age and the desire of many to shoot. However, where it offers little quality of animal life or fair sport, and where it devalues the land farmed by tenants because the birds become a local vermin in epidemic proportions, the question must be asked whether he has his priorities right and has thought it out. Government policies may suggest the opportunity and market forces dictate an expediency in reaping what others will spend on sport. Yet it begins to appear that although he is the owner he is not the complete master of his destiny. How well does he steward his property in the end and what are his options? The laws of nature dictate the acceptable side of dominion. Some like the Rev. Dr. Linzey *25 would argue that Genesis 1.29ff mean man was intended to be vegetarian to eat no meat, yet by the same token the following verse would suggest the lion and tiger should be too! More important is the hint of the sanctity of life in all that has the "breath of life" and how man values it and harnesses it in subduing the earth and having dominion over its animals *26 The breath of life is God's gift through creation and His to dispose of or control by whatever agency He decides.

As to the inviolability of private property and inheritance 1 Kings 21 speaks very soundly with the example of Ahab getting his hands on Naboth's vineyard. Commentators and thinkers like Sir Thomas More *27 and others have upheld the rights of ownership but more besides hangs there from. Hobbes stressed that the stability of society rests upon the consent of man accepting the status quo of ownership. Man likes adventure but he also likes to be settled with somewhere to hang his hat. Locke *28 cites that land is given by God to man in common. The search for other alternative uses and the sharing or letting of shooting is one aspect of how all might have a share now Winston Churchill's exhortation is overfilled. Bentham *29 saw just ownership to be based on labour. It stands to reason that without labour the asset of land is wasted and a man's property is nothing. At least it is what he can manage.

One of the most obvious ways to become aware of God's providence is through working the land and harvesting. The harvest of the sea and the experience of the elements come a close second. There is a sense that through the increase of the land the economy springs from nothing. Add labour and skill and soon there is surplus to sell at a profit. Farming and set aside and fallowing involve basic stewardship of the land and the environment in their respective ways. It is hard to detect where God's favour particularly rests and whether rewards are comparable to effort or care but a look at Cain and Abel*29 give a clue to what response God likes. There is an illustration of the measure of how much each loved God in the proportion to the time that their respective occupations and involvement with the land demanded. Both depended on the elements and water. Cain had more spare time having cleared, ploughed and sown his land before harvesting. Shepherds like Abel and early Israel were in service the whole time. God's delight with them was the greater and no doubt their awareness of him increased. The message of good tidings of great joy came to shepherds first then second to wise men as they followed their deductions and observations. *30 In a similar way the credit of being recognised as a countryman by one's fellows also reflects an acknowledgement of love of God's creation.

CHAPTER 2

Alternative Options

(i) Responsibility and Property Ownership

"The only ethic worthy of the dignity of man is that of love".
George Thomas

"Take not away the life you cannot give: For all things share an equal right to live".
Ovid.

Whilst man's duty to his fellow man is the first call or priority of his relationships, he will show himself in poor light for bad husbandry and poor stewardship of God's creatures. "Old King Cole" may call for his loaders three and blast away at the game in Edwardian style but if there is no feeling, only pure slaughter, he only serves to demean himself. Mrs. Thatcher *1 quoted four basic principles gleaned from George Thomas *2 "People have priority over everything else in God's sight. Every man has a value beyond price because he is a child of God. Because of man's exalted value, the mark of a good life is that of service to other people. The only ethic on which service should be undertaken and the only ethic worthy of the dignity of man is that of love". She would replace the notion of society with that of environment. If man is not a good steward of his environment he hardly maintains God's creation in a fit enough state to nurture his fellow men and successors. The government would hardly function without the assistance of charitable organisations in many different fields but charity, or love and care, must extend to the stuff of the world too.

To own property brings with it responsibilities and how they are exercised is an expression of character. So the theory of property, as being essential to full citizenship, is tested two ways. *3 Is it enough to live off? How does it reflect the personality of the owner? The first is the cause of extensification, diversification, intensification or whatever elsification may be fashionable to agriculture. For the most part farmers are conservative and follow the paths and innovations of their forefathers. Variations on the second extend beyond the conservative according to the means of the owner. Lady Balfour *4 followed and encouraged the development and practice of organic farming. She saw essential links between soil-plant-animal and man and the need to treat the soil as a living ecosystem to maintain suitable agriculture. She formed the Soil Association in 1946 having previously started the Haughley Experiment, a whole farm dedicated to organic farming research. The Prince of Wales' private organic garden at his house at Highgrove *5 is another example but with his private income he can afford to maintain his ideas and innovations through the expensive initial years of low production.

Canon Henry Scott-Holland *6 argued private property is conditional and not absolute. It is a social system where the personality is freely expressed. We have access to ownership or share ownership within the overall responsibility of a community. We are accountable to the absolute - God. The private estate must be the best example of this and where there is harmony and industry there is nothing to hit the headlines and draw attention to itself. Like marriage being the only good example to itself so too is the good private estate or farm. When it comes to sport and shooting the privacy of the estate becomes more public. It involves its own community but also draws in outsiders who inject other money into the whole business enterprise. (See Annex I & II).

I would like to share the joke of the farmer who, having won a lottery fortune, was asked what he would do. He replied "Carry on farming until I've used it all up". Maybe a cynical view, now in 1996, but it sums up something of the ethos of the landowner who puts something back into the countryside and what the various policies deluged from Brussels upon him cost.

2(ii) The Economics of Plenty

"The resources of the earth should be used as God's gifts to the whole human race and used with due consideration for the needs of present and future generations" Archbishop of Canterbury and others Times 21 / 12 / 1940 and echoed by William Temple in Christianity & Social Order 1942

Why has there been a turn around in agricultural policies or the overall strategy that can allow such diversification? Before the first world war Britain relied on imported food and industrial production covered the deficit it made on the economy. Two world wars necessitated home production to be self-sufficient and after 1945 Britain could not afford to import food on the same scale. *7 Government policy set prices and types of crop for 50 years. Agriculture became an industry. Food is relatively now far cheaper than before. In the 1930's half a man's wage was needed to feed his family and bread without dripping was probably the normal fare towards the end of the week. Government grants and subsidies enabled investment to produce more food. Even the E.E.C. complies with a policy of quantity rather than quality.

Against this necessity farmers are now accused of damage in producing plenty. Larger machinery requires more space. Much loved hedges were ripped out and if lucky small diamonds of trees were allowed on the corners of the prairies where machinery could not get in. Science was applied, so different strains of grasses and cereals were available. British bread is now from British flour. *8 The technique and unnaturalness of the system is now questioned. *9 As there is growing support for organically grown and healthier food with better flavour rather than for chemical food, the policy of cheap food may fade and food will have to find its own price. This will cause some to go to the wall and others to intensify once more. The soil is now five times more fertile. Harvesting is speeded up twenty times. £40m p.a. turnover in agribusiness: Tinsley specialises in vegetables and employs 1000 people. *10 The heat and light conditions for 13m chrysanthemums are controlled by computer. Harvesting and milking are possible by robot manned machinery. Cows can even be milked on their demand, to enjoy a lactation as if suckled by a calf. Pigs can be fed on demand by a computer programme that adjusts their amount of feed according to demand. Birds and beasts enjoy heathland welfare but perhaps not natural conditions.

Biotechnology does tinker with the stuff of life. We may see less controversial spraying, because it can be replaced by natural poison in the plants to combat pests and parasites. Cattle with B.S.T. in the pituitary gland produce 20% more milk. The life of the cow is shorter but A.I. ensures a more regular quality in compensation. Indeed animals are cloned so you get eight identical sheep that can be genetically "farmed on". One result of all this is that an increase by one farmer specialising and using new scientific technology, puts a handful of others out of work. If the extent of our Dominion is to reduce life to a mere chemical level and man along with it, all sense of value and sanctity is thrown away. With cash flow difficulties in farming, the result is the larger concerns do better. Many small farmers commit suicide. *11 The strains of big business also produce their own casualties. *12

For many average farmers shooting is basically another commercial venture with relatively low capital injection, depending on how much he does or charges others for, like many other forms of diversification. "Set aside" seems very much a wilderness that is the residue of present economic forces and equally evident in the U.S. In some ways the "wilderness years" following the Exodus of the Israelites from Egypt can be seen as a relevant comment on the situation where the farmer has to start from scratch after economic downfall. God provides the raw materials and the farmer has to sort it out and work with nature and creation.

It would also be appropriate to add some comments from a dissertation by John Rendall (A Theological Appraisal of the effects of Industrialisation upon the Rural Area), *13 He underlines the respectable aspect of farming whereby money from other sources is used to subsidize it, notably pension funds and individuals with other assets. I would disagree with his conclusions. There is self-interest involved but that is true of any aspect of wealth creation in a free economy. It must be argued that shooting as a form of self expression must be high on the happiness-making stakes, (it is a recreation) but at the same time shooting demands co-operation and conformity to maintain high standards and a good public image. All the more credit must be given because shooting has to dovetail into an industrial environment dominated by man's need for food. Indeed it has become an industry itself, although its product is usually associated with luxury. Certainly shooting does not destroy but controls and encourages the species hunted. Therefore within the context of shooting the rich cannot pursue their sport at the expense of the welfare of the poor. If the sport is conducted with dignity then the Church must recognise this and the part that shooting plays within the ecology of living creatures and stewardship of the land.

2 (iii) The Options of Farming Today

"Where we sowed our champion barley seed, darnel and wildoats choke the furrow. Where sweet violets and narcissus grew thistle and thorn are growing today". *Virgil Eclogue V*

In the light of set aside as an alternative land use for agricultural purposes there are a few options open to farmers.

1) Increase shooting and use the natural habitat to encourage and hold game for sporting purposes.

2) To leave land fallow or rotate a percentage that is left fallow in the spirit of Exodus 23 v 10 and time honoured farming techniques.

3) To put less into the land or production by way of bought in nitrates and accept lower yields and slightly less overheads.

4) Conservation, which often goes hand in hand with item 1), depending on attitudes and interests of owner.

5) Some form of organic farming or a change to what is locally most appropriate, although again this can lead to a difficult drop in income over five years or fifty five years in the case of woodland.

6) Try a selected high cash crop, such as old English roses for the extraction of scent oils for soap or perfume.

7) Convert land and buildings into recreational use for residential purposes, a retirement community or rest home, or holiday cottages. Golf courses, leisure centres, riding stables, sports centres, Deer parks, Safari parks etc, although as an alternative the first are becoming more controversial and a planning issue. *(Times 1-8/9/90)*

Many of these may seem inefficient or selfish in the face of a demand for a world economy based on a policy of plenty for all. Butter, meat and grain or apple mountains may disappear but where is the store for a rainy day? Joseph's stores were not so much surplus but a careful saving. *14 Here was no fiddling of prices and there was sufficient for the poor and needy.

The Somerset Levels *15 are a wetland now farmed traditionally or in the conservative sense of what was technically possible 100 years ago. However this and other Environmentally Sensitive Areas do add or reintroduce advantages to the community. With the willows once more pollarded there is a revival in basket and wicker work. The local farmer does not see himself as a "park" keeper as if there has been some organised "time warp". If anything the area is more reminiscent of Holland where all these traditional skills continue and the locals still carve out and wear clogs.

A policy of organic farming abandons the concept of cheap food, but many are prepared to pay more for wholesome food. *16 Part of the expense is that the system is more labour intensive and has a lesser yield but in the long term it is being found that where manures are compatible, and "friendly" crops grown in rotation, quality and yield increase

On the coast of Scotland and in some of its lochs there is an increase in Salmon Farming. This is often too expensive for an individual and at present there is real concern about the pollution it causes.

One person on the Mull of Kintyre invested his money from the sale of a shipyard into a hydroelectric scheme that supplies the national grid. One spin off was a source of spare warm water that was ideal for breeding salmon and even other varieties such as lobsters and oysters. The same principle had been applied for some years to farming king prawns at a mill in Yorkshire. *17 Perhaps if they had utilised the warm water from Drax power station earlier it might have been more successful, because the nearby tomato farm has harnessed the same resource very effectively. Will history repeat itself? The locals in the Selby area before 1914 went on strike about being fed salmon more than three times a week! (However one local trawler owner who remembered the incident suggested it was because they only got the head and tail pieces).

Germany after the war had nothing to lose and is now enjoying the beech woods planted so extensively as a public amenity but also for hunting. Sadly few in England consider their grandchildren, except for tax purposes, yet we import 90% of our timber needs. *18

Straw burning is now discouraged and may contribute to the excess being made into paper with a new mill being made in Yorks. However the 40 year return on softwoods and 120 years for broadleaf trees is discouraging. There needs to be more encouragement besides for the landscape and the part they play in the conversion of carbon dioxide into oxygen and the evaporation of moisture drawn from the ground. *19

Those who prefer to harvest holidaymakers instead of hay make a good living if they have initial investment or sponsors, although set against the cost of a combine the initial outlay may be available anyway. Alton Park, Lightwater Valley, Beamish Museum, or enterprises like Longleat Safari Park also prove educational. *20

2 (iv) Set-Aside or Diversification?

"The earth has yielded its increase; God, our God, has blessed us"
Psalm 67:6

Is set aside really part of conservation or economic mismanagement? Yes the land needs rest or at least not relentless cultivation that puts nothing back. Witness the sharp decline in the graph marking a return on land cleared of rain forest in the W. Indies or Amazon areas. Crown Estate Commissioner and Gloucestershire farmer, Oscar Colburn, *21 draws attention to new markets awaiting our food exports, yet imports of the same account for half our adverse trade balance. It needs the drive of something like B.F.F. year to encourage the housewife to buy, cook and serve up more game in place of the plastic-tasting, water-injected chicken available in so many supermarkets. Mr. Colburn is more pessimistic "about micro-biology, genetic engineering etc., being translated quickly into higher output at farm level". *22 He observes that farming as an industry owes the banks £7 billion, the interest on which is a serious burden to any farmer (bar my next door neighbour who owes nothing to any bank and whose equipment is similar to that used by my grand-mother when I was a boy). As a direct result future investment in farming as a business is likely to be nil for some time unless farmers can sell their produce at their price.

Furthermore the age range of the average farmer, 50% being over 50, adds to disincentives to make changes and invest heavily. That production will not continue at the same level also seems likely. The decline in the number of available tenancies affects ownership and use of the land adversely blocking the way for younger men into the industry. *23 As agricultural economy becomes less stable there is a tendency for landowners to sell land, *24 manage land directly, or enter into share farming agreements rather than renewing long term tenancies. 1971-86 shows a decrease of 10% in tenanted land to 50%.

It therefore follows that if farmers can make money from D.I.Y. projects like shooting they will do so in order to cream back some of their money that flows into the city on the loans they have had in the past. As people like to identify with the country and its pursuits the city types will gladly pay for what is offered them. Farming, unlike many other enterprises, has to have an eye to the welfare of future generations so its policies span two or even three generations at a time. This is an aspect on which conservation must depend, as ultimately stewardship is about handing something on in good working order, including the basics of soil condition. Naturally this produces objections or reactions to certain current practices. Intensification is not popular. Conservation is about maintaining a more traditional animal, for instance , rather than one bred to meet certain conditions. Little bacon today is from Gloucester Old Spots *25 one of the traditional house pigs in the back streets of industrial housing complexes. Straw burning is a necessary part of the intense modern farming cycle and it needs more than regulations to encourage straw to be used in other ways, not least being the economics of the operation. No doubt the world without the hand of man, despite his mistakes, might be far more polluted. We do see straw used to make artificial hedges or windbreaks in pheasant woods when higher ground can be used. *26 However banning straw burning can lead to an increase in the use of agrochemicals etc., costly to the farmer. Burning also destroys weed seed, and on the moors heather burning encourages heather growth, whose seed needs fire and frost.

Organic food immediately sounds attractive with ideas of natural food, naturally produced, and free from chemicals and additives. Less weedkillers on the crops, more wild flowers and better taste like the raspberries mulched in the kitchen garden on grass cuttings and horse dung. Mr. John Gummer has announced that M.A.F.F. is now sponsoring research into aspects of organic farming and one vehicle of help is the European Community's extensification scheme. All this has overtones of conservation and raises hopes of a better environment for grey partidges and all. Even human sewage can be better processed and treated to make up for the deficiencies and lack of natural fertilisers like dried blood. *27 If farming faces a slump there may be continued pressure to cut silage as fast as possible but hedges can be restored and stubble left after harvest as spring corn and less roots are grown. Again this would encourage the same partridge but as a totally wild crop. *28 Equally as important to conservation from the shooting perspective is an attitude not to kill what will not be eaten.

The N.Y. Moors National Park Plan Consultation Draft goes into some detail about "extensification or low input farming over large areas having beneficial environmental effects" but mentions nothing at all about shooting or job creation and the earning capacity of shooting. Yet this goes hand in hand with its view that farmers would become both environmental managers and food producers. The Association of National Park Officers produced two reports *29 suggesting this and proposing that a system be devised "that treats environmental management as a crop". Shooting is too sensitive to mention, yet if the bracken is more harshly controlled (no longer is it used for bedding beasts and cut as a matter of course) and replaced with sheep on the heather the grouse will suffer. The report does sound a caution that the trend towards ranching may accelerate the loss of landscape features, and reduce employment opportunities "through extensification". Furthermore the growth in part-time and "hobby farmers" which may or may not include some shooting could lead to pressure for new development and land use changes on such newly created small holdings in the area. This brings money into the area but little extra work and means that farms and buildings sold for housing are too expensive for locals to buy and develop.

The report further mentions that "Diversification" in farming by setting up recreational facilities, pony trekking, golf courses and other outdoor activities or other types of farming like fish farming can adversely affect landscape, the water quality and wildlife habitat respectively .*31 It also advocates setting up workshops and low cost houses for locals to encourage crafts but has not the money to fund it, over 50% of its present budget being Government grants. Even where the N.Y. Nat. Park spills over into the parish it can strangle private initiative with its planning regulations that border on "preservation" rather than conservation as we tend to think of it. A famous wood, for instance, painted by a famous artist needs to be managed if future generations are to see the original landscape for themselves. There is such a strong attitude to preserve such things that they are in danger of being lost completely by not being touched at all. Imagine if everyone wanted the subject matter of their holiday snaps preserving for posterity!

Whilst on this note it is useful to contrast how other organisation manages similar landscapes. The Army Ranges at Warcop face a high ridge in the Pennines north of the A66. Traditionally ranges are grazed by farmers with sheep at their own risk. In fact few animals are lost but trees are because they nibble off any self-seeded saplings. Most of the range is a safety area so nature runs its own course with whatever help an interested party may give it. With initiative from the Commanding Officer, who enjoys his field sports, woods in the safety areas have been fenced to keep out the sheep, so they have regenerated and spread a bit further. As there is also undergrowth other wildlife (and pheasants and therefore shooting) has settled there. Small ponds have been created that have been stocked so local angling clubs pay to fish and subsidize any improvement or management. These in turn attract wild duck for shooting but also provide reservoirs in case of moorland fires. Essentially there remains a varied habitat that gives pleasure and provides sport and sustains the effort needed to manage it. This same point about a varied habitat was made in an article that wildlife thrives where there is room for a hedge or two, which intense farming does not allow. The article *32 was about the Army Ranges at Foulness where there was much wildlife, including migrating birds in passage but there was a need for the sheep to be reduced in number and excluded from certain areas. It was no coincidence that I was at Warcop when the article was published and immediately saw the benefits of a little sheep control during the course of my duties as Yeomanry chaplain!

Lastly how the N.Y.M. Nat Parks can manage to confine "intensification" of farming to land of low ecological value, *33 including bracken invested areas with little potential for other uses, remains a mystery. One of the few non-capital intensive schemes for such areas can be the creation of a shoot for pleasure and / or some profit, as a hobby by a group. *34 One parishioner with the capital to do so from a business he sold has made a very reasonable sporting estate and farm on the edge of the N.Y. Moors, out of land he has had to reclaim in part in such a way as described.

At the moment when the noises from Brussels are reasonably sifted and filtered it appears there is less involvement with conservation than there might be and less interference with shooting as it exists. Most of the directives are concerned with meat hygiene and this only applies to wild game if it is processed and dressed. Any inspection is likely to be on a random rather than regulated base because of sheer logistics and costs. "Going bingo with the Community" as David Curry M.P. *35 says, "involves co-operation, although a wary eye has to be kept open to notice any extreme suggestions or unrealistic ideas that may creep in." As in any bureaucratic society wishful thinking of any ideal needs support and cash to put it into practice. If either is lacking then those who dream up the schemes may as well shout at the wind. As it is there have been inspections and strict regulations on venison and deer carcasses for some years. Such a reality gives some indication in calculating where the majority decision in Brussels will fall in proposals relating to wild game and shooting.

2 (v) Theology of Set-Aside

"the Earth is the Lord's and the fullness thereof, the world and those who dwell therein" *Psalm 24:1*

After a service one farming parishioner remarked that while it was good to have prayer for farming and harvesting etc., we should have included "set aside". He feels "set aside" is an unrealistic approach for farming and that the scrub which unused land becomes is a poor advert. "Set aside" may produce a better income for the farmer with poorer land but it leaves a lot to be desired. My next door neighbour who fallows land as part of his rotation cannot afford to "set aside" 20%: he would rather see all farmers encouraged to leave land fallow on a subsidy basis. For the conservation minded "set aside" may appear a good policy but if only bad land is "set aside" little will be achieved. Unless what is "set aside" is rotated as fallow little extra wildlife will survive. If policy is changed and land is required for cultivation, it will be sprayed heavily with chemicals. If rotated some of the accumulation of acid will have time to leach out and wild life will spread itself. Furthermore there is still the temptation to "set aside" some acres and claim a subsidy and artificially increase the yield on the remaining acres with chemicals.

I speak as an amateur in these matters but there is a theological precedent we should consider. What the Bible has to tell us is based on experience and understanding of God's will and it would not be too disparaging to say that it adds up to sound common sense! Amongst all the laws and commentaries found after the giving of the law to Moses in Exodus 23.10 are references to a sabbath year every seven when the land shall be rested. Certainly the land needs a breather and the benefits are obvious. At this time the Israelites were in a state of transition from being shepherds to being settlers and landed. By leaving land fallow there was an opportunity for the shepherds to graze it so the whole community was supported.

Alongside this was the custom of redeeming those fallen on hard times and returning land leased out, partly to ensure that the owners remained the occupiers. Every fifty years was to be a jubilee year, the once in a life time redemption and a time for making new contracts (Leviticus 25.8-24) and settling old ones and leases. This also served as a census year when each man had to return to his tribal area. It is an interesting thought that every six years the Lord God will bless the land so it yields enough for the next three years until the harvest of the eighth year is ready. What farmer sows today with that thought in mind? During these sabbath years nothing was tended. I can hear the cries of "one year's seed means seven year's weed". As we do not live in a theocracy today such injunctions may seem irrelevant but all the same they are food for thought.

We can derive guidance from another Biblical character too. Joseph fixed the land policies for Egypt, Gen.47.13, as a result of Pharaoh's dream, Gen 41.25 becoming reality. Thereafter everyone saved a bit. The ancient myths of Egypt reflect the interaction between the Nile flooding and famine or plenty.

Less than a century ago grain was not threshed until it was required or the price was right so there has been a policy of storing always. A store is not needed just to keep an artificial price but also to provide when there is need. Whilst grain mountains have diminished and sighs of relief are heard, is it not wise to lay up something for hard times? Having met the Minister for Agriculture I am assured that there is sufficient time to grow the necessary extra and with a world wide economy this can be achieved in less than a year. Not that I want to record a general discussion word for word but I still have reservations that Biblical wisdom and the experience of history are being neglected. What if the new-sown corn elsewhere is drought bound?

Nature and man, indeed the whole of God's creation, is very adaptable to conditions, both good and bad. Instead of being poisoned by the pewter of his drinking vessels man is now realising the damage of his leaded petrol, though not before he has prepared a generation of engines really capable of using unleaded fuel. Instead of exhausting the land, crops are rotated to revitalise the ground, though methods in Latin America leave much to be desired. However the urge to make more money does make man squander land by opting for cash crops rather than a more natural or suitable crop which sometimes is not even food for himself! So perhaps rather than set aside we could see trees grow where trees grow well, corn where it does well, milk from pasture land and meat where beasts thrive. Sharing the whole of creation and its resources applies today as much as in the times of Joseph and his contemporaries, hence the motive behind God's laws.

The Royal Agricultural Society of England have sponsored the production of liturgies along the traditional agricultural cycle themes - Plough Sunday, Rogationtide, Lammas and Harvest Thanksgiving. *35 These in themselves build on the imagery of what the agricultural industry is doing at the time and did historically (spraying and praying at Rogationtide!) and provide straight forward spiritual truths. It would be good to see churches buying these booklets and hearkening to what God is saying to us through the mud, toil and sweat of working the land. Perhaps we should "set aside" ourselves for deeper reflection on being stewards of God's creation and keep land in production more gently to regenerate itself?

Lord Caldecote in a series on wealth creation and the Church makes the point that over the years the Church has hallowed the industry of agriculture where evidence of God's providence is more obvious but has failed to do the same with Industry in the modern sense. That same industry creates wealth and provides the wherewithal for many, not least currency for recreation and freedom from drudgery by modern technology. Yet the Church scorns industrialists with its socialist ethos that money-making and capitalism are wrong,which is one of William Temple's sadder legacies. *36 As shown already there is nothing wrong with wealth and wealth creation, but there is the pressure and expectation that "of him who has much, much is expected." Currency is a means of expression. The challenge is that expression is godly. Again Temple did not enquire too deeply into how wealth was created, although it served to help and care for the weak and disadvantaged. It is also worth considering that the brewers started the Temperance Society not to encourage teetotalism but to offer a more suitable alternative to gin. Human nature goes so far, the church challenges it to go further.

Other observations are worth including at this point (1996):
1) Compared to Europe and the States this country boasts no industrial dynasties, or industrial aristocracy, in any numbers. Instead the tendency, on making any money, has been to invest it in land and embrace that way of life. It may be more expressive, and, indirectly, is also one of the sources from which many of our national artists are nurtured or patronised, but serious lack of investment in industry results. Such investment via industry might perpetuate more efficiently some of the larger estates.
2) Taking a sabbatical break in working life is proving very beneficial to those who take it.

CHAPTER 3

Shooting and Farming

"The land shall not be sold in perpetuity, for the land is mine, for you are strangers and sojourners with me. And in all the country you possess you shall grant a redemption of the land".

Leviticus 25.23-4

(i) Shooting and the Community

In 1809 Sydney Smith took up an incumbency at Fosten-le-Clay, York and shepherded some 300 souls. *1 He used a telescope and an immense speaking trumpet to farm a similar acreage of glebe. I'm quite sure that many of my predecessors over the years have advised and co-ordinated their contemporaries long after the days when the plough was no longer kept in the church. Nowadays most farmers or land owners have been to Agricultural College or similar and are very professional. The churches in the parish are very dependent on their support, be it in kind or cash. *2 For the outsider the church remains as a reminder of being the guardian of better values. Through the priest and in worship the farmer is still reminded to be thankfull *3 for what God provides and services such as Plough Sunday (Jan) Rogation (April 25) Lammas (Aug 8) and Harvest Thanksgiving (Sept - Oct) express and illustrate our part in creation. *4 Now that less than 2% of the working force in the country work the land, farming is a lonely job. *5 Local radio and C.B. radio chatter are little compensation for the past companionship of others or some horses. Shooting days provide a pleasant break from a lonely routine and offer fellowship and a chance to chat whether at the level of Gun, Beater, Picker-up or Driver. Here, as much as the market place, news, prices and other information are exchanged. Shooting is very much part of country life and is here to stay, drawing in many with no agricultural or landed connections.

Most would accept that land, or property, is owned on trust from God and comes from Him. *6 This in turn suggests a natural order of responsibilities that we are stewards or tenants charged with the care of creation. God's provision extends to all things for all people, so ownership has a communal reference prior to any private one (Access, thoroughfares and provision for recreation are immediate illustrations). Private ownership makes relative sense so that things are better administered for the social whole and so a man can support his family's and dependants' basic needs. God's other gifts enable how this is achieved because what is earned comes from a combination of talents, abilities, intelligence and social setting. Wealth, whether cash or soil, is not for hoarding but is a vehicle in existence precisely to enable the bearing of fruit. (Described earlier even as a test or time of trial!) Retention of what could be given or provided for those in need is immoral, being lack of charity, an act of injustice. Such an attitude can be viewed as even theft and possibly murder. Mammon means "In what I trust" and if wealth is the sole extent of someone's trust they are the poorer for it. Aelred, to whom a bell dated from 1350 in Leake church is dedicated, which may come from Rievaulx where he was Abbot 1147- 67, commentated like many others that land was held in trust and did not have to be given away literally. Those without property and possessions were alike challenged to give what they had, prayers, alms and help to others. *7 If the source of help was material it still had to be run and administered.

A modern view is summed up as well by Pope John XXIII as anyone. *8 "In defending the principle of private ownership the church seeks an important ethical and social end. She does not intend merely to uphold the status quo..... nor protect on principle the rich and powerful against the poor and indigent she aims at securing private ownership precisely according to the plan of Divine Wisdom and the dispositions of Nature". Private ownership is seen as a guarantee of basic freedom and an indispensable element in true social order. State and other public agencies ought not to extend their ownership beyond what is clearly required by the common good.

(ii) The Economics of Shooting

"Some people get on terms directly; but in return give a great deal of themselves away, as fast". T.E. Lawrence The Mint p161

Shooting on private property clearly does not infringe the common good. Individuals may like it to excess as much as others find it repellent. Such is human nature. National laws govern some of its conduct. The "Field" makes suggestions for a certain common approach by common consent. *9 The support for the sport depends ultimately on its participants playing the game and observing the practice of their forebears. Those brought up from an early age to handle a gun properly usually have the most consideration for the sport, the bird and the public image it projects.

Shooting at some commercial level may be necessary to sustain a farm or provide cash flow in what has become capital intensive. When working out the inheritance and a policy for his estate a cousin of mine drew three circles on the map. (1) round the house and park, basically Elizabethan. (2) round the outside perimeter of the estate. (3) somewhere in the middle of the other two including the traditional "home" farm. His reasoning was that if necessary - recession, economic collapse, mistakes by his son, - the outer ring could be sold to maintain the inner two for a generation. If things continued badly the middle ring could be sold off to maintain the centre as a unit for at least a generation with no other income in both cases. Shooting therefore, and it is good shooting with high birds out of trees above low valleys, or rough shooting and wildfowling in other parts on the river, provides a necessary income. Alongside the shooting forestry goes hand in hand, but as a long term policy, so the two complement each other. Another hope is that in lean times other assets can be realised (One great great grandfather was a patron of Canaletto 1697-1768 and had a considerable collection which were sold to pay death duties 100 years later or so; such collecting or capital investment could be repeated).

Lastly of course the current owner or his heir could exercise some skill or vocation, be it the traditional soldier or as a lecturer in economics, (his elder daughter is!) that would provide income and an individual pension further enabling the estate to be handed on intact for posterity, generation by generation.

In view of the limitations to income because of market forces and over production (but not on a world wide scale) for farming, the bad image of "set-aside" and its low or regressive yield, shooting is a real possibility for many as a cash crop that even the staunchest conservationist has to accept. *10 Certainly there can be too much of a good thing, especially where pheasants reach epidemic proportions and cause damage, but it is a sport that can be conducted at many different levels according to the means of the participants or in return for what an owner is prepared to provide or allow. Many of the happiest shoots are on a "do-it- yourself" or part-time basis and rank as a complete year-round hobby. The most exciting can be the rough shoot or quest for the wild birds rather than those put down and keepered.

"It may be that shooting has been going through one of those undesirable hypes which have been a 1980's feature. They are the artificial working up of a cult, sport, or activity as the "in thing" for those who have neither real roots, basic instincts, nor knowledge that goes deeper than such superficialities as merely knowing what a peewit is. *11

"If so the 1990's may see it readjusted so that nationally we return from hype to reality and follow the inclinations which we actually have, as distinct from those which we feel we ought to have because other people profess them. The effect on shooting would be a shake-out from the currently amorphous shooting community and its reduction to those who find in it - improbably as it may seem to some, but wholeheartedly as it would be to most - their contact with Creation." *11

The future of shooting does depend on attitudes and how people discover themselves through such contact with creation but at the end of the day it is and remains an opportunity, God given, to discover and express the self. The bird pays no more penalty than it normally would when subject to the forces of nature. Indeed the culture of society raises its esteem as art and writing illustrate.

(iii) Shooting and the Future of Farming

"In the northern parts of the island, in the Peak District, stags have become so numerous in our own lifetime that they have been known to charge hunters with their hounds and trample them to death". Gerald of Wales Description of Wales *Bk I ch 8 p235*

From a conference on the ethics of modern farming practice some pertinent points can be applied to the consideration of shooting as a farming alternative or part of farming itself. Generally we need to replenish the world. Life is about survival. Our faith urges us to ensure survival of others and God's creation. The land needs rest and should not be overburdened. *12 Some of the pressure would go if other countries were encouraged to be self- sufficient in their food production. Nature's own way provides game where there is food for it, be it little or plenty, man provided or fallow, so shooting will always be part of the ecosystem for food, sport and remuneration in that order. Shooting can be considered an aspect of natural man if free to do his own thing. It is his expression alongside the exercise of his responsibilities and through it his attitudes, motives and response to God can be measured. There is a caveat from Fr. Thomas Cullinan that sufficiency and self-interest are signs of an atheistic society. Shooting at its worst demonstrates this but that is cause not to stop it but to encourage people to find a higher level of expression through it with adjustment of their attitudes and horizons.

Considering that the world food reserve is only some 15/45 days *13 should we take life more seriously than shooting pheasants? The world is a difficult place to organise as God knows! Science is improving our productivity. Even the corn we think of as indigenous, and the green blade for the fowls of the air, is a hybrid of the rye variety introduced centuries ago. Unless pheasants become staple food for some reason we are unlikely to see the breed of a super bird.

If too plump they do not fly so well! However science can ensure better health, better use of resources, better performance and, if we are scriptural in our attitudes, better allowances for others.

Shooting as practised today, (and those who do not play the game are soon spotted and ostracized!) can be said to preserve the freedom of the animal. Reared birds are free from hunger and thirst, disease and fear if properly released. As Prof. Spedding continues they enjoy shelter and have the freedom to display normal behaviour patterns. If we are to see the world restored to one view *14 of how God's vision of order and peace is worked out then not only must man become vegetarian but the lion must conform too or become extinct (which is hard luck on the browsing elephant now poached to near extinction for its tusks unless genetic engineering comes to its rescue).

It is thanks to shooting as much as other aspects of farming that we enjoy the landscape as it is and are likely to see hedgerows flourish and enjoy the prospect of gamebirds in the wild. It is thanks to shooting that there is a real contact or involvement with nature as man becomes progressively more technical, concrete-bound and removed from the outdoor scene in everyday life. It is thanks to the challenge of shooting that man can work out his values and attitudes and response to God. Hopefully however man tackles his use of land, however he farms the soil and however he has dominion over the beasts of the field and the fowls of the air, he will be aware that before God "Thy will be done in earth as it is in heaven".

(iv) Shooting and Set-Aside

"Pleasure is what you remember of an activity, i.e. what you remember you've shot, 25-35". *Maj. Gen. Sir John Acland, The Field*

If "set aside" of arable land is an option taken how can the farmer who can put at least 20% of his land down to "set aside" make it pay for doing nothing? £80 an acre may be a good subsidy but he will have to spend £20 an acre on maintenance if it's not to be a wilderness of weeds. Syndicating a shoot may give some extra income if he has over 250 acres and the shooting rights or teams up with neighbours to make a suitable shoot. He could otherwise grow hay for horses which is compatible with maintenance and shooting. When one is to consider that retreat mining in the Selby Coalfield that is capable of producing the entire national need, wastes 40% of the coalface and abandons what were left as pillars during the mining of the rest, it would seem that even "set aside" need not be wasteful overall.

Of the possibilities and returns offered to landowners inclusive or exclusive of "set aside" on their land, shooting is the most likely to be lucrative assuming a suitable size and seclusion for safety reasons. Indeed shooting is an industry and an earner of considerable foreign currency. Unless bureaucrats in Brussels become too bullying the U.K. offers better shooting possibilities to the sportsman than anywhere else in Europe. *15 In the interest of fair play and a good name The "Field" has drawn up a code of practice to encourage voluntary restraints against overkill. Shooting will be profitable for the smaller landowner if he acts as his own agent to let it or as his own keeper to run it. Even the Forestry Commission can make money out of pest control by culling deer and selling venison meat, by letting stalking and letting shooting rights.

In comparison with the shoots described and emphasising the industry of the enterprise a shoot in the parish that has gone commercial now fields three keepers as it did fifteen years ago. The difference is that the family that owned the estate then employed them to preserve and encourage existing stock and had a few pheasants under broody hens. The emphasis was on vermin control and managing habitat and rides when shooting took place. The modern keeper today constructs pens, puts down or rears totally something in the region of 11,000 birds and feeds them heavily. *17 He is more of a poultry manager. Whilst obvious vermin control may take place he feels the stock put down is sufficient to cover some loss to vermin - foxes, mink, stoats, rats and other predators besides magpies, jays, rooks, hedgehogs and others that steal eggs from the wild nests. *18

CHAPTER 4

The Ethics of Shooting

"The fear of man lays a snare but he who trusts in the Lord is safe" *Prov.19.25"*

(i) Shooting as a Sport

As already suggested *1 man has an instinct to hunt from the earliest days of his development or evolution in order to feed himself. Meat is a source of protein and in winter when vegetables are less available primitive man found food on the hoof and killed it as required. Documentaries on life in the jungles of the world illustrate that man remains a hunter. In part therefore those hunting instincts remain with the more domesticated and industrialised man of the twentieth century and find expression through hunting on horseback or on foot with hounds of various description. Others go either as a single gun beating up his own hedgerows with a dog for the occasional bird for the pot, or as a wildfowler or pigeon shooter. Yet others will form a team or syndicate on an organised shoot for wild or reared pheasants and some partridge, or on the moors for the grouse or blackcock. *2 The motives are twofold: one is the enjoyment and pleasure of the chase as a pastime. It is recreation after work. It is being out and about in a natural environment away from the office desk or modern machinery. It is sharing in a natural cycle of culling game and providing for the table, and there is no doubt all game makes the best eating, to say nothing of the wild extras like hare, woodcock, and snipe. Rabbits, as a result of myxomytocetes induced to reduce numbers, are no longer popular cheap fare. Yet when prolific landowners used to be notoriously mean about allowing people to shoot them despite food shortages. As the hare eats one third the amount a sheep does some culling is necessary.

The second consideration is money. People make money from providing or organising the sport. Few rural communities have been without the traditional keeper in one form or another since the introduction of the pheasant from the East in the seventeenth century. Indeed, as said elsewhere, *3 the formation of sporting estates has done much to preserve the countryside as we know it and wish to keep it. Many ancillary services also benefit from the shoot: there are the beaters who enjoy the bonus whether farm labourers, miners, or wives with dogs; the hotel trade, who provide accommodation and food; the manufacturers of 4WD cars where the real use of a cult vehicle is still to be found away from the King's Road in London. Add to that the manufacturers of guns, sporting gear, cartridges etc and there is a major industry. However banning or curtailing shooting would not put all these out of work, for there still exist gun clubs and competitive clay pigeon shooting is an Olympic sport. *4 If there were to be national or E.C. limits on shooting game there would be a howl of dismay from the conservationists who realise that much of what they want to keep or preserve is because it is "keepered". Some may want to stop shooting to improve the morals of humanity. *5 It could be argued better that restraint of a more voluntary nature is better for humanity. Over indulgence is the ruin of a good thing, especially where there is too much emphasis on enjoyment and pleasure. The old saying "everything in moderation" or "a little of what you fancy does you good" rings true.

Lastly, despite the arguments of Andrew Linzey,*6 there is no prohibition on eating meat, Gen 9.3(1) builds on the provision given at Gen 1.29(2) and Gen 2.16. Indeed the difficulty of catching game for food still exists and the most humane way on average is with a shotgun. Furthermore in line with Gen 9.4 a shot and dead animal does bleed from sheer blood pressure being released and any visit to an abattoir will illustrate that meat has to be bled if it is to be tender.

(1) "Every moving thing that lives should be food for you; and as I give you the green plants, I give you everything"

(2) "Behold I have given you every plant yielding seed which is upon the face of the earth and every tree with its fruit; you shall have them for food"

(ii) The Need To Shoot?

(1) "One man is proud when he has caught a poor hare and another a little fish in a net . . . . are these not robbers?"
Marcus Aureleus (121-180) Meditations.

(2) "He kept fat partridges in coops."
The Franklin; Chaucer's prologue to Canterbury Tales.

The next consideration is the tension between need and greed. Ban shooting and all incentives to encourage and preserve game birds are lost. Some culling would still be necessary, whether for damage control like the squirrels in Kew Gardens, *7 or to limit the number of cocks so time and energy is not spent fighting each other but breeding. For the poor farmer or tenant the bonus of game on his land to supplement his larder was useful but often limited by law. With enclosures from medieval times onwards he was even more restricted in enjoying these extras. *8 Game laws were in existence restricting the right to hunt to those whose property was worth 40/- per annum. In 1671 it was set at £100 for freeholders and £150 for tenants. As a freeholder even the vicar or rector enjoyed some sport, although his curate would depend on his largesse to improve the meagre fare of his table. Where the landscape was unenclosed poaching was prolific, although commons and wastes were not considered "no-go" territory. Sometimes the less scrupulous landlord to improve his shooting impaired the value of the land he rented out by swamping it with birds or planting game shelters. The Prince of Wales in 1863 was a particularly bad offender in his attempts to raise his annual bag from 7,000 to 30,000. "Strips were cut across my fields like a gridiron and planted for game shelters .... until the trees were sufficiently grown .... noxious weeds grew .... no-one being allowed to cut them for fear of disturbing nesting". *9 Vanity is far from being an argument for need! However there is a reasonable point at which the landscape can be managed to encourage habitat and facilitate sport for the future. It is based entirely on human consideration for others and the game in question. Anything done to excess is undesirable so the way forward must be pragmatic.

The only consideration for need to shoot game is that of obtaining them for food. Reared, released and in the wild until shot, they can for the most part enjoy a natural life and a sporting chance. *10 Shot and properly hunted up and collected with dogs trained for the purpose there is very little suffering involved *11 and certainly no more than being caught by any other predator. The value and pleasure of working with a dog adds to the sport and quality of life of many people, including those who do not actually shoot. Finally on greed it must be stated that most shooters have a natural revulsion against excess. *12 Excess and greed bring in a bad name for the blameless but the dividing line is extremely thin. God provided for the needs of the Israelites in the wilderness with manna and quails but those who collected or ate too much paid the penalty! *13 The Field published a recommended code of practice: *14 no birds to be released after start of shooting season: no more birds to be released in the area than what that same area would naturally and healthily hold. Other considerations fill out the picture: i.e. caller birds should not be held for partridges after the initial release. Duck should be wild enough to get up off water and perhaps with the emphasis on shooting them flying back rather than away. That a bag of 500 should be sufficient is another suggestion for the pheasant shooter and a policy of not shooting a single drive more than once a week. *15

Shooting can be seen as an opportunity for sport into which many have thrown themselves. It also gives people a chance to express themselves for better or for worse and use their hunting instincts rather as a young Masai warrior may still seek to kill a lion with his spear. Greed may increase as need in the form of commercialism to earn a living diminishes. It is never easy to sort out people's motives when set against their values and the incentives, for the argument can go either way. The lure of a high bag may attract guns who are prepared to pay more. The same line may also be the incentive for greater gains. With the practice of tipping the keeper and perhaps also paying according to the total bag there are two considerations. One is the incentive to collect up as many wounded birds with good dogs. The second the temptation to bump up the bag by ruthless feeding or taking in a release pen so the birds are pre-gathered in an area where shooting will take place ensuring a larger bag.

iii) The Respect For Animals

(1) "Until he extends the circle of his compassion to all living things, man will not himself find peace". *Albert Schweitzer*

(2) "Moral education is about finding within us an ever increasing sense of worth of creation". *Dr. Andrew Linzey. Animal Rights SCM*

Thought must be given to the esteem in which the quarry is held. There is an inevitable harshness in nature and that side of creation. A study of prehistoric cave paintings or aboriginal art or bushmen's lore puts a challenge before us as to their purpose. For the most part they depict a reverence for the quarry and much wishful thinking. If something is enjoyable it finds expression and needs passing on to others. In a similar way the wealth of sporting prints and art today expresses the same. *16 The pleasure of the sport, the esteem in which the quarry is held, something of the means and trappings of the sport and how it is done and a wish to be at it more often, all stop short of actual worship. Even the birds of paradise are comestible!

All of God's creation is of special value to him. *17 "Are not two sparrows sold for a 1d?" We are of value to God too, (Luke 12.22-34), more than sparrows. Even these do not fall to the ground without God's will but in the fall of game do we acknowledge God and are we accountable to Him? If we are considerate rather than callous there need be no fear of retribution. To love a child does not prevent smacking it if the situation warrants it. To love creation does not exclude eating and enjoying it so long as we are reasonable. The world is a testing ground for us all. The real sadness is those who credit animals with attributes they do not have and either debase humans to animal level or raise animals to a level of some sort of graven image for worship. The domestic pet suffers more than most along with anything in captivity but there are few action groups with that cause in mind and Greenpeace is not noted for picketing old ladies closeted with their cats.

Much is to be learned from nature, or out and about doing something, be it bird watching or gameshooting. It is awe inspiring and poses questions for the sensitive person to try and answer. Job and Elihu admit they learn from nature and know another aspect of God. *18 God, in turn, enjoys response to his creation. Study of the same in the birdlife alone teaches man aspects of himself. *19 Study of their life cycle also illustrates where man can help to his advantage or destroy through his greed. Thus the considerations for the conservation aspect are very variable.

Whilst the bureaucracy in Brussels may baffle some and ban *20 some sporting practices it is a useful melting pot of ideas if not allowed to get out of hand. It is healthy that we question our own practices and remain sensitive. By comparison with habits abroad we appear to be playing the game very properly and sport in the U.K. is much sought after by foreigners prepared to pay well for it. We do not have thrush pate on our menus but in Corsica it generates a turnover of some £2.5m from some 10,000 lbs of the product. Hungarian pheasant farming has already been mentioned.

The spirit *21 of how we conduct ourselves and how we determine limits to our behaviour are best taken from seeing the world in the context of creation and our accountability to God for our stewardship. As stated in my contribution to the debate on the ethics of the sport (the worst offender has clearly been the day release shoot where the bird has had no consideration or chance) the biggest problem is greed. A fellow contributor with whom I once soldiered would also like to see people playing the game properly, "so that the sport is conducted with respect, decency, mercy to living creatures and dignity by the participants". *22 He could well quote the psalmist *23 that if the sport is seen in a bad light by the public the participants will be digging a pit into which they fall before they have time to dump surplus game that has lost its commercial value, or is badly damaged from been shot at from too close by.

Andrew Linzey questions the hierarchy of being, but criticized Christians for having no satisfactory moral theology on animal treatment. *24 Indeed in Catholic moral theology animals are but brute beasts with no understanding, therefore they are not persons, and have no rights. Even Francis of Assisi draws conclusions from animal observations but in no way seeks to impose human qualities on them. As quoted in his "Life" by St Bonaventura "If you have men who will exclude any of God's creatures from the shelter of compassion and pity, you will have men who will deal likewise with their fellow men". It is one thing to observe life but another to impose upon God's order of creation man-like qualities amongst the animal kingdom. Descartes accepts "that we cannot prove there is any thought in animals. I do not think it is thereby proved there is not - for the human mind cannot reach into their hearts". Richard North in the "Animals Report" observes that "as animals feel pain like us we must respect them and their feelings". *25 In 1964 the report of the Committee on Cruelty to Wild Animals (H.M.S.O.) makes several observations and sees nothing to prevent shooting. 131 The misconceptions of opposition to field sports are based more often on lack of knowledge. 136 fieldsports attract tourists. (The increase since report written proves this). 19 There was much reaction in favour of rabbits but non for rats!. (How childlike we are, perhaps!) This report concludes it is more decent to hunt for food and fun even though the vegetarian is free to say the former is unnecessary and those who do not enjoy it the latter.

(iv) Conservation Hand-in-Hand with Shooting

"Animals are helpless and dependent on us. They are trusting therefore we have a responsibility not to neglect them nor violate them by cruelty" James Herriot "The Extended Circle" *(Edited J. Wynne-Tyson.)*

Few would deny that any work enjoyed by an individual ensures a better job done. Farming has a very mundane and lonely side that is compensated by moulding the landscape and enjoying nature and organising sport and recreation within it. Thus whether it means planting trees and hedges for wildlife, using less spray on headlands round the edge of the fields to encourage wildlife, etc., the rewards of doing that or being able to capitalise on it to some extent are part of the incentives. To see and encourage wildlife is as pleasant as shooting it! It is uncanny how many pheasants come out of hiding after shooting stops on Feb 1st! That would not be a sight for people to enjoy if there was not a real element of conservation in shooting, along with better managed woods and rides. Often the Game Conservancy gives very good advice on how to manage game and farm at the same time. "Rare wild flowers, butterflies, animals and wild game have a better chance of surviving and flourishing on arable land than at any time in the last 40 years". *26 All this is the result of greater public awareness and co-operation. The Cereals and Gamebirds Research Project started in 1983 is one such response resulting in greater sensitivity to encourage the indigenous grey partridge. This is done by helping chick survival during their first two weeks through ensuring a greater insect density on the field edges and by reducing or using specially selected pesticides which do not break the natural food chain. The cost in a 40 acre field of winter wheat where 6% has been left as a conservation headland would be a reduction in yield overall of less than .05%

The Game Conservancy Objectives are: (1) That populations of game, wildfowl, deer and fish should be conserved and husbanded at densities which allow cropping on an optimum substantiable basis in a way that is sympathetic to other users of the countryside and which benefits game, the natural environment and rural communities. (2) That game conservation should be regarded as a valid use of sustainable natural resources and valued as a prime example of conservation through wise use. The dependency of use creates a self interest on the part of the user in sustaining the natural resource and in defending it from unwise use or destruction. *27

Such objectives as outlined by the Game Conservancy reflect dependence and acceptance of multiple land use. Users therefore have a responsibility to ensure that wild life can co-exist with their activities; usually agriculture and forestry. It upholds a policy of rearing birds for release in areas where they could not be managed otherwise. At the same time it disapproves of any practice or behaviour that brings shooting into disrepute as this threatens the future of one of the incentives, shooting itself, and the management of the habitat on which game and wildlife depend. Again thanks to the Game Conservancy there is better keepering which is more informed, trained and less prone to the blinder traditions that could otherwise persist, so that predator control is better without leading to extermination. *28 Again the habitat for all wildlife benefits. In other respects grouse stocks are preserved as the lesson is driven home that they suffer from overgrazing by sheep as does the heather itself on which they depend for food. It is hardly surprising that the staunchest conservationists have to grudgingly admit that shooting is on their side and serves the same interests. *29 Grouse apart, flora and fauna in many shapes and sizes and in various and differing parts are encouraged and preserved as a result of such efforts because the environment is maintained in a more friendly manner without being too green. When people go over the top David Sinclair sounds the caution that "the buzz- word "preservation" should be confined to jam making". *30

N.B. (1990) As this is printed, there is an offer under consideration from the Game Conservancy to offer farmers a subsidy on sheep on grouse moors should meat subsidies by the Govt. be lifted, as already an increase of sheep numbers has drastically reduced grouse stocks in some areas.

(v) Theology and Shooting

(1) Thou shalt not kill. *Exodus 20.13*

(2) "I am in favour of animal rights as well as human rights. That is the way of a whole human being". *Abraham Lincoln 1809-65*

It would be foolish to overlook what is implied in the Ten Commandments. Certainly the Sixth Commandment is not a chapter for vegetarians, although some would take it as such who have not explored deeper. Stuart Blanch *31 in his delightfully simple exegesis explains the word "kill" as meaning if translated literally "dash in pieces". Thereby is implied rage or temper, a hasty reaction or cold blooded revenge. Clearly it is an act totally lacking in love and forgiveness. When spurred to Holy War no quarter was given by Israel, yet even Samuel had to slaughter the Kings that Saul had spared. Their blood was God's and He required it. *32

Two points emerge from this. In considering shooting the act itself is not a breach of this commandment, despite the association of guns being used to slaughter faithless partners and their lovers.

The second leads to a more serious consideration: the sanctity of life as being precious to God. Reading the O.T. God would sometimes appear rather rapacious for blood and only to be appeased by sacrifice. Yet Saul's disobedience prompts Samuel to explain *33 "Has the Lord a great delight in burnt offerings and sacrifices as in obeying the voice of the Lord? Behold to obey is better than sacrifice and to hearken better than the fat of rams...." Even this message got through to Israel and Jesus encountered the response "and to love him with all your heart.... and to love your neighbour as yourself, is much more than all whole burnt offerings and sacrifices" .*34

In the O.T. the principle of life is declared to be in the blood (Gen 9.4). As no atonement for it is possible without the sacrifice of life, the blood shed on the altar is a visible representation. "For the life of the flesh is in the blood .... it is the blood that makes atonement by reason of the life". *35 Thus God could see life was given by the presentation of blood, as was evident on the cross once and for all. Leviticus goes on to teach "For the life of every creature is the blood of it. Therefore you shall not eat the blood of any creature". *36 It was the forbidden portion, whether of fowl or animal. *37 Blood was symbolic and its significance lay in a relationship to God from whom life came. Thus today the Jews and others slaughter their animals in a particular way that others find abhorrent. However if you slaughter, say, your Christmas turkeys, it is no good strangling them. They have to be dispatched and bled otherwise the flesh is tough. This can be done cleanly so that the blood runs to the head when the bird is hung up and plucked and is then disposed of with the head when the carcass is drawn. Certainly a bird well and cleanly shot through the head will be killed instantly and naturally bled for the best flavour.

Although it may seem a great jump I can see no reason for prohibitions on shooting for biblical reasons. There is no ritual sacrifice about shooting as a sport nor does God set aside animals for any religious reason. As to blood shed in field sports there is no embargo on it for the theft of God's property. If any parallel is to be drawn it is that of conscience. In the days of sacrifice what was not offered on the proper altar but in shrines of man's erection was invalid and the blood guilt was upon the culprit's head. In a similar way slaughter for the shooter's gratification can be seen as blood guilt upon his own pate. Indeed everything that lives and moves is given as food for man now. (Gen 9.3)

The fundamental point is the consideration of the quarry and of other people and their interests. Consider Psalm 24 1-2 "The earth is the Lord's and the fullness thereof".

SUMMARY

1) Shooting helps conservation. Indeed on the grouse moor it is a form of conservation.

2) Shooting provides real contact with creation and sharpens our responsibility for nature.

3) We are not exclusively vegetarian. Game provides a good diet and shooting is as humane as any other man-made system of culling animals.

4) Shooting and land or property are an expression of the personality, usually for better than for worse!

5) Shooting shapes the landscape that people know and love being a motive and incentive to plant trees, root crops etc., most advantageously to game.

6) A varied habitat sustains wildlife and gives pleasure. Sport provides the incentive and sustains the effort to manage that same habitat which would otherwise disappear without grant aid or being exclusive through having to charge visitors.

7) Whilst shooting and conservation go hand-in-hand animal welfare is a separate issue. In any reasonable setting no animal suffers any more at the hands of man than it would otherwise in the wild. Many fare better. Man is still part of that same chain of nature and creation whatever other ideas of grandeur and ideals he may have!

8) If land is not to be farmed how else can it be used? Recreation is the name of the game.

9) Ownership of land is a form of service. Can love be shown through owning land and through shooting? In what perspective does property put Justice? Land ownership is part of man's expression, and his relationship to God.

10) Shooting and foresting can go hand in hand and be ecologically helpful.

11) Prov 6:5, Eccl. 9:12, Amos 3:5 and the parables of Jesus (Matthew 10:29, Luke 12:6) are all pictures drawn from life, accepting a status between man and animals. Gen 25:22, Esau and Jacob, illustrates hunting in the Old Testament.

REFERENCES

Chapter 1

1. R.E. Howard-Vyse Langton Historical Notes of a Village
2. Aristotle Politics
   Aristotle Metaphysics
3. Politics II
4. G.E.R. Lloyd. Aristotle: the growth and structure of his thought.
5. Exodus 21:2, Deuteronomy 15
6. Exodus 23:10
7. C Rowland. Christian Origins SPCK
8. V. Bartlett Property Ed Gore 1913
9. Psalm 95 (Venite)
10. Leviticus 25:10
11. 1 Chronicles 29
12. Proverbs 30:8
13. Malachi 3:5
14. Matthew 25: 14-30
15. 1 John 3:17
16. C. Gore Ed. Property
17. Hegel Life of Christ
18. BBC2 Television Programme July 3 1990, entitled Present Imperfect: Lord the Land, on Mr. Buitelarr, near Louth, Lincolnshire, see Appendix 2.
19. C. Gore Property
20. Aguinas Summa Theological
21. Williamson and Bellamy Property and Landscape Philip 1987
22. The Countryside Commission Policy Document May 1989
23. The Field Summer Special Edition 1990
24. C. Gore Ed. Property MacMillan 1913 25. Genesis. 4:1-7
26. Luke 2:8-20 Matthew 2:1-12

REFERENCES

Chapter 2

1. 17 January 1990 Details of N.C.H.G.T.S. Conference quoted in The Times
2. Viscount Tonypandy, former speaker of the House of Commons
3. C. Gore Property
4. Lady Balfour. The Living Soil Faberf 1943
5. The Times December 1989.
6. C. Gore Property
7. Great Yorkshire Show statistic. Before the War over 50% of beef was imported. Now Britain is 92% self-sufficient.
8. Same statistics
9. Rowlett Centre, Colchester, Essex
10. The Silent Revolution BBC1 Television Programme 16 & 17 Jan 1990. Now published by BBC.
11. Peter Warren. Stress Among Farmers Hull University MA (TUIS Course) 1990, quoting the Samantans, Northallerton
12. Many of these statistics were quoted at a study day at Stoneligh, RHM Centre, May 1989
13. Hull University MA 1989 (TUIS Course) Conclusion, quoting Perspectives on Economics C.I.O. Pub 1984.
14. Gen 25: 27 ff
15. The Silent Revolution.
16. " " "
17. Was Croysdale's Mill. Now R.H.M., Whitley Bridge
18. Silent Revolution
19. Young trees use three times the amount of carbon dioxide whilst growing to maturity.
20. The Silent Revolution
21. The Field March 1990
22. Ibid
23. Ibid

24. North Yorkshire Moors National Park Plan (Draft for consultation, farming section) March 1990
25. Andrew Patterson 150 Years of Farming Rare Breeds Society B.F.F. 1989
26. Bertram Sample. "Farmers and Pollution" The Field March 1990
27. Dr. Paul Hadley, Reading University, Conference, Stoneleigh, Dec 15 1989 and David Bellamy BBC T.V. Tomorrow's World June 1990
28. B. Sample, F. Fulford, W. Stevens The Field March 1990
29. The Association of National Parks Officers National Parks at Risk 1987. National Parks-Environmentally Favoured Area 1988
30. North Yorkshire Moors National Park Publication
31. Ibid
32. Ibid
33. Shooting Seminar, York, February 19, 1990, Colonel C. Egerton
34. Same Event
35. The TimesMarch 13, 1990
36. William Temple Nature, Man & God, 1934
Christianity and Social Order 1942

That Temple was a card carrying member of the Socialist Party for a while shows his ability to get stuck in and alongside what is happening. Like R. Niebuhr he was not one to dodge controversy and be content with shouting from the touchline.

P.S. By 1996 straw burning has been banned but the straw accumulates. I've also not the time nor the space to comment on B.S.E. amongst cattle other than the obvious folly of feeding meat to beasts that chew the cud, worse still that the mixture contains other beasts of the same species. See Leviticus in passim.

REFERENCES

Chapter 3

1. The Smith of Smiths Ed. J.L. Carr, 27 Mill Dale Rd., Kettering.
2. Unless totally offended by ill-considered debates raised at General Synod like the proposal to ban hunting on Church Commission land, which could not be implemented anyway. July 1990. They have bridged the contradictions between creation and stewardship.
3. Lord Caldecote. The Times 13.3.90
4. Farming in Britain Today B.F.F. 1989 Celebration
5. Preface to Country Services Booklet. Sponsored by the Arthur Rank Centre, Stonleigh, during B.F.F. year 1989.
6. Preface. Thomas Cullinan, O.S.B., Ownership Lace Benet, Liverpool
7. Aelred. Rule of Life (Notes to his sister)
8. John XXIII Pope 1958-63. Quoted from Ownership. He is also quoting Pope Pious XII.
9. Summarized June/July 1990
10. The Field November 1989. Simon Barnes "The Times" 8.11.89 "Shooting & Conservation".
11. The Field November 1989
12. Sir Peter Mills, Ex M.P. S. Devon. Arthur Rank Centre, Conference Stoneleigh
13. The then Minister of Agriculture in discussion with me at the G. Yorkshire Show July 1989. John Macgregor
14. Revd. Andrew Linzey (Also he and Prof. Spedding were on "Arena" T.V. discussion animal rights 16.12.89)
15. See notes on shoots Annex I & II
16. As has another shoot owned by a parishioner but on the opposite side of the Moors
17. One shoot owned by Arabs in Norfolk puts down 60,000 birds

18. No comparison would be complete without mentioning the local oral tradition that fondly remembers Canon Kyle who lived and ministered on the N.W. corner of the North Yorks Moors two generations ago. He bought up much farming land and woodland during the inter-war years slump which he shot over and conducted most of the rest of his ministry in the hunting field on horseback. He also bought the village pub which caused remonstrations from the Archdeacon to which he replied "How else can I ensure it remains closed until evensong has finished?"

Consider the old tale: A vicar complimented a gardener in the village on what he and the good Lord had achieved in harmony together. "Aye" replied the old man, "but thee should ha' seen it when the Lord had to 'issen."

REFERENCES

Chapter 4

1. Gen. 25:27 ff
2. Not to mention shooting deer for food and export in Scotland, or to protect young forestry
3. Williamson & Bellamy Property and Landscape
4. Field Magazine 1989 - 1990
5. The Times Article by Simon Barnes Fri. 11th August 1989
6. Andrew Linzey Animal Rights SCM 1967. He cites Gen 1:19 as meaning we should all be vegetarian along with some ecologists who see Christ's redemptive act stretching even to the soil itself. Compare Revd. Echlin, Christian Green Heritage Grove Booklets. For me the green plants referred to in Gen 9:3 are those in the Garden of Eden at the start of Creation, Gen 1:29
7. Spring 1990!
8. Property and Landscape P.198
9. Mrs. Creswell 18 Years on the Sandringham Estate quoted in Property & Landscape
10. See letter by C.J.R. Pope in Appendix
11. See article by me in The Field May 1989
12. Ibid
13. Exodus 16:13, Numbers 11, Psalm 105:40
14. The Field November 1989, March 1990
15. Ibid and Code for Good Shooting Practice B.A.S.C. and B.F.S.S.
16. See "Snaffles" prints, on the work of Stubbs, Lional Edwards, A.J. Munnings and others.
17. Matt. 10:29
18. Job 7, 35.11
19. Article on pheasants, back number of The Field by Lord Ridley's son

20. The Field November 1989. Shooting Seminar. York 19.2.90 Sportselect.
21. Own article The Field May 1989
22. Sir Watkin Williams Wynne, Ibid.
23. Psalms 91:3, 119:110, 124:7, 140:5, 141:9-10, 142:3
24. Andrew Linzey Animal Rights SCM 1967 Christians and Animal Rights SPCK
25. Richard North Animal Rights
26. The Game Conservancy, Fordingbridge, Hants
27. Game 2000 A manifesto
28. Proper courses now run at the G.C. School in Hampshire
29. Simon Barnes The Times 11.9.89
30. Shades of Green, Myth and Muddle in the Countryside
31. For All Mankind
32. 1 Sam. 15:33 and Gen 9:4 ff
33. 1 Sam. 15:22
34. Mark 12:33
35. Leviticus 17:11)
) All reasonable commentaries
36. Ibid 17:14) Will expand on life blood in the
) light of the atonement. i.e. Alan
37. Ibid 7:26) Richardson A Dictionary of Christian
) Theology S.C.M. 1968 and below 2 - 6

(2) Karl Barth The Doctrine of Reconciliation 1956

(3) John Macquarrie Principles of Christian Theology 1966

(4) Leon Morris The Apostolic Preaching of the Cross 1955

(5) Paul Tillich Systematic Theology II 1957

(6) F.R. Barry: The Atonement Hodder & Stoughton 1968

Farm and alternatives

Size 1350 acres		180 acres	Winter Barley
		288 acres	Winter Wheat
94 acres grass = 200 ewes		28 acres	Oil seed rape
rest = scrub / woodland = pheasants		470 acres	Spring Barley
		(could not plant winter crops in time)	

Altitude 1050' down to 750' = gill bottom 450'

Cost £5 - £10 per acre + £5 per acre to clear / reclaim 1926 / 46
A hill subsidy on rough ground would only provide 10 cows but too expensive to fence

Yield 2 ton wheat per acre £98 net / ton 10.10.88 (Peak year '85 £100 a ton)

Cost £70 per acre (equivalent to £50 / acre since '85).

Fixed overheads of machinery = Grain dryer, 2 combines, 5 tractors etc
Labour 3 / 2 men (x1) + owner 1 tractor costs £35-40,000 (x2)
4 cottages 2 / 1 for workers
Buildings etc

Alternatives:
Problem on marginal farms to find / create higher returns. With "Set-aside" subsidy not to grow corn £80 an acre may be available but it will cost £20 an acre to maintain land and no stock or commercial use allowed. If land left fallow it would be ideal for partridge, which like stubble and weed, and pheasant. This would make it a commercial prospect in itself because the area is big enough for a shoot and the gill is ideal for keeping and presenting high sporting birds over guns.

The Shoot:

Started with owner and friend walking up hedges and rough ground: about 40 wild pheasants a year. So they put down some birds and formed a private syndicate.

74-75 season:

Friend brought in 1,000 6 week old poults. 7 days shooting 7 guns total bag 539 (100 a day) No extra employment. birds fed by shepherd, feed bought from farm by owner. 5 ton wheat per 1000 birds.

84-85 season:

Rear 2,500 birds and share a keeper with another farm/shoot. 9 days shooting Nov-Jan 31st av. 240 a day + 1 let day £16.50 a bird. Syndicate still private: 4 members + their guests pay £2,200 each. 7 guns: 10 beaters: 2 stops: 1 driver: 2 paid + 3 vol pickers up + dogs. Keeper + house + vehicle costs 2 shoots £10,000 p.a. Costs £10.00 per bird shot (value = £1.00 to butcher!). Incubator 2nd hand £1,500: 2 hatchers 2nd hand £750. March - May - June: Catch/hatch/rear/release pheasants.

Future: Double birds put down and let 7 - 8 extra days to 8 guns at £3,300 per day.

Notes: x (1) One man just finished: not replaced.
x (2) Cost of tractor = value of agricultural house.

In 1995/96 these figures have changed:

Stock: On 94 acres of grass there are 320 ewes

Arable: 187 acres Winter Barley
365 acres Winter Wheat
183 acres Oil seed rape
223 acres Set-aside

Yield: 3 tons Wheat per acre @ £100 per ton

Cost: £100 per ton

Machinery reduced to 1 combine and 2 tractors
Labour: 1 man and owner

4 cottages: 1 for worker, 2 let out and 1 empty

Set-aside subsidy at £100 per acre

Birds are costing £17-£18 to produce.

Future: Quadruple number of birds put down and let extra days at £5,500 per day (approx £700 per gun)

Total price up by £10,000

ANNEX II

Farm:	6,000 + 750 woodland + let and other 5,500 acres		
Shoot:	9,000 acres 12 days	1,000 acres let to another neighbour	

Income from shooting

Game sales: 3,000 birds (£1.50 per bird) net of VAT during season
Sell 5 days £3,000 per day to Americans Company & Corporate structure (10 nights x 14 people £14,000 -in Estate House + 3 days grouse + pheasant (NY Moors)

Costs: '89	2 keepers	14,000	Income for
	vehicle p.a	3,000	estate from
	4,500 poults mid July	9,000	sold days can
	" " food	3,000	be as much as
	Sporting rates on not		£20,000 less
	in hand land	400	costs to estate
	Beaters	3,000	office in organising
	Lunches/expenses/staff	1,000	and running
	Rabbit gas	1,000	it etc.
	Artichokes/netting for		
	pens	1,500	Cost £20,000 to
	Total	£35,900	estate '87-'88

Benefits: Vermin control 1/2 time work of keepers (Feb - July)
Extra income from 2 let guns 1,500
Syndicate shoots 7

Conclusion: Pheasant income pays pheasant costs.

Without shoot:

Still 2 men + vehicle + costs for rabbit control 3 acres of corn round each wood lost Miximytosis recurs when numbers increase

Rabbits at 25p if anyone will buy them now.

How it affects farming cycle

Small areas of game plots / strips / dead ground
Banks fenced off. Spring barley headlands not sprayed
Conservation good. Stubble left where possible for spring sowing. Weather controls game: '88 good weather for partridges 1st hatch: bad weather for partridges 2nd hatch

Damage Control

Shooting happens round farm and forest
£300 p.a. Roe deer. Keepers + owners do most of it.
1 wood replanted 3 times 3 years running 15 acres of hardwood saplings tipped out. Squirrel damage to 20 year old trees, hardwood. Bucks April - Oct: Difficult in summer 4 shot. 16 Does and calves £30 - £50 carcass

2 YTS lads on keepering from B.B. Ag. College

Injection of $ without shooting would not happen. English corkage on wine imported would be expensive to raise similar income!

Topography dictates where pheasants are put to present high birds.
Now 21 different drives 200 birds a day (700 wild birds)
Making room for foxes: avoid release pens to keep hunt happy x 2 a month during season over estate.

Neighbouring shoot:

40 days over 4,000 acres: 900 a day \ man made vermin
20,000 pheasants put down.
Such numbers become man made vermin and annoy tenants. Sole reason is commercial.

5 year period:

Set aside min 20% of land 900 acres: £80 per acre. This would loose 1 farm manager: 3 farm men: 1 keeper. Fixed costs £120 per acre therefore £90,000 to manage + 1 combine / 3 tractors £20 per acre to manage set aside fields.

April 89 a farm comes up 280 acres
No sons / neighbours interested
This could be "set aside" as a separate entity within company
Plant clover on it
Game strips if place is right
Stubble

Cycle of production / shortages:

'84 European bumper harvest. 2% VAT to EEC covers overheads of food storage for West. Is EEC a food policy or a social policy?
Agriculture affected when things are short or surpluses happen higher prices for Scottish lamb is an instance of interference by Govt. policy to agriculture finding its own level.

EEC = a bigger purse: agriculture needs support to maintain workers' standard of living. Meat eats corn so affluence wants more bread! therefore support food prices to maintain a tractor driver on farm.

Compare:
Russia: food sufficiency ever? North America: soil erosion terrific
U.K.: fens shrink, clogged, and this is sunken land too!

U.K.: Wolds erode
India: Deforestation causes floods - rivers filled more quickly, water level rises in Bangladesh estuary unless dredging takes place, because water runs off more quickly in Nepal.

Seed & harvest time:

84 good: 86/87 bad

Technology needs a good man to work it: who makes man? if one man doesn't pull weight or share overtime (like foddering beasts) it makes more work for the others.

Why do it?

Owner's Stewardship

Part of Creation

The Estate is a Family Business evolved from Industry - (land bought with money in C16th from Nottingham coal mines,) innovation took place. Difficult to maintain as prices drop. Challenge to maintain family business employing 55 people Compare 3 circles round estate mentioned in Chapter 4

"Farm like mad and stand still!"

Owner's job has changed: Landlord to farmer since 1976.

"Dead" money tied up in housing for staff.

Socialist legislation, because small business unprofitable/not viable, caused most change and destroyed "socialist" outlook of care and cottage

Moral responsibility for staff: pensioners who are housed along with employees.

Weather is Act of God! (or fault of man?!) '88 July bad therefore spring barley prices bad

Church= neutral. Within the estate there are 3 of 5 parish churches in group.

2 vicars: 5 churches: not supported exclusively by estate: Church is the people but not enough involvement + Methodists. Local church issues: Conflict - no change (Older generation).

Small numbers therefore have - shorter services? (attract younger generation).

Population in 3 villages c300. 10% go to church, but farm men work Sundays.
In villages "dead" land could be sold for development.
In 1/2 one village and in 3 others, less policeman's, the Estate owns all houses. Main historical change came with regular employment not weekly /annual. They would have been housed en famile but now with their families. New skills, not ongoing acquisition of knowledge like a horse, have to be learned beforehand.

Only 2 farm men don't deal with stock. Radio York is the only companionship during 8/10 hr working day against horse of 60 years ago which needed another 4 hrs of care and attention on top of working day of 8/10 hours.

Conclusion

Satisfaction of running a team/producing crop/earn living!!/ enjoying environment.

1995/96

Game sales down to £1.00 per bird

On solo days:

Accommodation at £120 per night (x7) for 14 people.
All costs have doubled.
Now 3 keepers
5000 poults at£11,000
Feed costs the same
Rates have doubled
Rabbit control costs increased by 2.5%
Beaters only cost about the same (£16 x 12 people x 15 dogs)
Game crops costs = the same

Details of a grouse moor N.Y. Moors

Area 14,500 sq acres 3,000 acres of bracken to reclaim to make another drive. Av days shooting per year 23.5
35 beats, only shot x 3 each season
Bag 100 brace per day : 8 guns per day
Av shots per killed bird 3
Income £6,600 per day = £35 per bird or £10,80 per shot per gun
Rates are levied on numbers shot ? Poll tax!!

Workforce 3 full time keepers. Maybe two more trainees by 1992
Cost of running moors to tenant £80,000 p.a. including time spent clearing rubbish, maintaining access and paths which public also use. Heather burning also benefits sheep farmers!

Bag for 1989 Season 1,300 brace.

From observed estimated average at start of 1990 season the author reckons 100 birds per beat. The first day was 96 brace and 4 young birds to 1 old bird on average on the higher moor (cooler and with water).

1995/96

Costs:	£4,000 casual labour
	£10,000 beaters (£500 / 20 days)
	£6,000 chiller to store fresh game
	£2,000 road upkeep / access
	£3,500 x 3 = rent for 3 keepers
	£22,000 bracken spraying
	£45,000 3 vehicles (Rovers) + tractor, 4WD
	3 full time keepers + 1 YTS trainee
	Same area shot over: brackenspraying added 2000 acres increasing grouse feeding area.

N.B. Even after aerial spraying more needs to be done over the next 4 years to complete effectiveness by teams on foot with back pack then 1 man with argocat. It will probably take 4 weeks of the year. Bracken used to be managed before 1st World War as it was cut for bedding and put under flagstones because the damp will not rise through it. Especially good for larders!

Average number of shooting days reduced, but bigger bags 12 days in '95, 17 days in '96. This also helps to reduce disturbance and hassle to the birds (except lead shot!)

New lines of butts put in but do not work long term as the old flight lines continue. However they serve to catch the birds out from time to time or provide alternative drives if wind direction demands it. Commercial pressure had resulted in the rape of the moor and 4 years up to '95 of a ten year lease nearly ruined the moor and drastically reduced stocks.

The aim is a bag, 100 brace per day = 12 brace a gun as a comfortable margin with plenty of stock left. In fact in '96 one week of 3 days at the height of the season the average bag was 200 brace, but conditions were good and grouse were plentiful, because the moor had been rested the year before.

Income works out at about £1,000 a gun with fixed rent up to 2000 brace for the season.

APPENDIX 1

Letter dated 5.2.89

I wonder if my ramblings are too late to contribute towards your thesis on commercial shooting? It would be lovely if you used it as an excuse to come here, in which case all our doings would be an open book to you.

I see an immense number of shoots with every degree of commercialism (few have none unless totally rough). The ethical decision of what is right or wrong here is a difficult one but I am sure it does not divide with the line of commercialism and there is an argument that greed increases as commercialism diminishes.

I believe the ethics of shooting require a concern for the environment; its existence should enrich other plant, bird and animal life, and it usually does. At least equally they require a concern for the quarry and in medium-plus scale shooting that has to be underwritten by the organiser through first class picking-up. Ironically if the fee for the day is variable with the bag (which some think artificial) it is a great incentive to ensure that all wounded birds are picked!

There is perhaps an ethical argument that shooting reared birds is better, being replenishable, than wild, where we have less influence on numbers. Some commercial shooting is of course of wild birds. One has to be careful not to try to prove the general point by the specific (non typical) example. There are examples of cruel, greedy, environmentally bad shoots, both private and commercial, as there are examples of cruelty to domestic animals on any scale down to the old lady who grossly overfeeds the peke! But all of the commercially successful shoots (with staying power) that I have seen have been good, or better. But I know of a private shoot where the numbers and quality would be repulsive to me; the common factor sadly is the early lack of understanding of newcomers, but honestly I think they graduate. We try to offer only the most challenging birds here with hopefully impeccable rules for the environment and quarry and we have a jostling queue waiting to come, at the top of the market price.

The greatest greed which I perceive is of rich people with private shoots who over indulge themselves. I do not see that it is greed to share it with others for payment.

My father would classify the money we generate on the shoot as vast riches. All the income does is to allow us to employ two exceptionally nice people, one with very happy family, and provide and maintain houses and vehicles reasonably well. To rear, keep and feed the birds in healthy surroundings, where they want to stay; to fell and replant bit by bit the woods, encouraging warm undergrowth; and finally to provide a few days shooting for our friends. The very last day is for the beaters, which is maybe the happiest of the lot and finishes with a great feast. Many more people get livelihood and fun from a well-run commercial shoot than from a weak private one. The only difference from the old days is that some of the money is new and less hidden.

Any help?

Yours Christopher.

Present Imperfect: Lord of the Land.

With Jeff Perks's film this excellent series moves away from gritty tales of urban deprivation for a portrait of a traditional English village torn by a row over a factory farmer. We are in the Lincolnshire wolds, where the vicar and squire are double- barrelled cousins and Tennyson tea towels are sold by the church in honour of the area's famous poet. Although no one is tasteless enough to say so, objections to the factory farmer seem partly based on his being an incomer, and Dutch at that. As villagers protest against pollution, increased traffic, animal welfare and the destruction of the countryside, the vicar refuses to take sides. He points out that many people owe their livelihood to the controversial Mr. Buitelaar. But the conflict is often no more than a framework for a presentation of local characters, the vicar's wife dutifully taking the role of unpaid curate, the middle-aged paper lady on her bike and Audrey the outspoken churchwarden.

Times: Whats on? BBC2 3/7/90

APPENDIX 3

A precept from a sporting parson.

As a Gun, beater, loader or picker-up, the Rev. Toddy Hoare puts the blame squarely on Greed, and quotes Genesis 1.

Being a parish priest in an area with several shoots, of which some are commercial, and having in the past earned my keep by beating, loading, or picking up, I am taking a serious look at shooting as an industry and its place in God's creation. Please permit a few thoughts to help people think things out.

Sometimes I am fortunate enough to be offered a day's shooting in place of a parishioner who cannot go, funerals permitting. I have a working dog trained by myself.

I am not impressed by the numbers of game. However, drives often take in a release point or feeding area so quantity can be bumped up. Therefore it seems the problems of field sports are greed, lack of understanding and feeling for the sport, and a failure to see the whole within the perspective of creation. Thus:

Lots of birds attracts lots of money and lots of money seeks lots of birds. Guns, shoots, agents, landlords and even keepers where the bag dictates the tip, can all be guilty of greed where demands are made in excess of Nature's norm. Private shoots can also be guilty if motivated for the wrong reasons.

The worst advertisements for field sports are those who do it without applying themselves to what it is all about. Money does not buy everything nor compensate for time spent as a youngster walking with an unloaded gun. Those sharp enough to make a quick buck should be sharp enough to learn the ins and outs of the shooting field.

We have dominion over the fowls of the air just as every green thing is there for them to eat, Genesis 1,24 ff. Part of our stewardship is to ensure their welfare. Originally, birds were put down to supplement wild ones within the limitations of what the keeper could catch up (therefore maintaining a balance in relation to his natural stock) and what his army of broodies could manage to hatch. Now it is so overdone in places that pheasants have become a man-made vermin.

Greed must therefore start where demand pushes limits beyond Nature's normal capability. The limits are God's barriers. Many recognise this unwittingly as their natural revulsion to overkill shows.

For me, the finest sport is stalking. But shooting for the pot may not be in the commercial line or appeal to those who do not want to abandon their Range Rovers.

The Field: May 1989

APPENDIX 4

Courtesy Yorkshire Farming Bulletin.

And All from a Football Pitch.

Farming in Britain 'went metric' with all other industries, and land is now measured in hectares. One hectare of farm land is equal to 2.4 acres, or roughly the size of a football pitch.

The amount of food which can be produced from that football pitch is truly amazing:

nearly 35,000 kilograms of potatoes, enough to feed 340 people for a whole year;

nearly 135,000 kilos of tomatoes if it was covered by glass - enough for 25,000 people a year.

more than 5 tonnes of wheat, enough to produce 6,250 loaves of bread.

19,000 pints of milk if cows were kept on the grass, enough to supply 1,000 people for a year, or 350 kilograms of beef, the amount 20 people eat in a year.

10 tonnes of apples from an orchard is one year's supply for nearly 900 people.

Within Britain there are some 18 million hectares of land used for farming, and what it all adds up to is this: every man or woman working in farming provides all the food eaten by 50 people.

British farmers provide consumers with plenty of food, a wide choice and freedom from shortage.

BIBLIOGRAPHY 1

General — Books

Aristotle — Ethics Penguin Classics 1953

Aristotle — Politics " " "

J.C. Atkinson — 40 years in a Moorland Parish Macmillan 1891 Rigg 1988

Thomas Aquinas — Summa Theologica 2:2 Qu.66:2 ref Gore, Property page 128

Lady Evelyn Balfour — The Living Soil Faber 1943

Thomas Cullinan O.S.B — Ownership (An anthology) Ince Benet, Liverpool

Bamber Gascoigne — The Christians Wm Morrow N.Y. 1977

Bamber Gascoigne — Ticker Khan Jonothan Cape 1974

Charles Gore — Property Macmillan 1913

George Goyder — The Just Enterprise 1987

T Hobbes — Leviathan

David Lee and Howard Newby — The Problem of Sociology Hutchinson 1983

T.E. Lawrence — The Mint Panther 1962

A. Linzey — Christianity and the Rights of Animals SPCK 1986

A. Linzey — Animal Rights SCM 1967

G.E.R. Lloyd — Aristotle C.U.P. 1968

J. Locke — Treatise on Civil Government Ch 5 pp 27-28 Grove Property p.43

W. Marshall — Rural Economy of Yorkshire Cadell 1788

D. McClellan — Marx Fontana 1975 (and others, same author on same subject)

G.A. North — Teesside's Economic Heritage Cleveland C.C. 1975

B. Reardon — Hegel's Philosophy of Religion Macmillan 1977 includes Life of Christ

C. Rowland — Christian Origins SPCK 1985 p.28
Anthony Russell — The Country Parish SPCK 1986
Adan Smith — The Wealth of Nations Penguin
Vernon White — The Fall of a Sparrow Paternoster Press 1985
Virgil — The Georgics Penguin Classics 1987

Biblical Doctrine of Man in Society

Stuart Blanch — For All Mankind B.R.F. 1976 The Ten Commandments Hodder 1982
J. Bright — History of Israel S.C.M. 1972
Margaret Kane — Gospel in Industrial Society S.C.M. 1980
H.R. Niebuhr — Christ and Culture Faber 1952
Peake's Commentary on the Bible
Social Institutions of Israel Nelson 1962
Harold Perkin — The Origins of English Society 1780-1880
William Temple — Christianity and Social Order Penguin 1942 SPCK 1976

Ethics

R. Preston — The Future of Christian Ethics SCM 1987
A. Suggate — William Temple and Christian Social Ethics Today 1988

Ministry

Aelred — The Spiritual Kiss vision of St. Aelred of Rievaulx Ed. Robert van der Wayner Little Gidding Press 1989
R. & A. Hanson — Reasonable Belief O.U.P. 1987
R.R. Niebuhr — Moral Man and Immoral Society 1932 Scriber 1960
R.R. Niebuhr — The Nature and Destiny of Man Hibbet 1941

Wider Reading

Jean Briand — The Judes Christian Church of Nazareth Franciscan Printing Press Jerusalem 1982

G.B. Caird — The Language and Imagery of the Bible Duckworth 1950

William Douglas Home — Sins of Commission Michael Russell 1985

Gerald of Wales — The Journey Through Wales and Description of Wales Penguin Classics 1978

Laurens van der Post — The Lost World of the Kalahari Penguin 1975

The Heart of the Hunter Companion Book Club 1961

Pierre Teilhard de Chardin — The Phenomenon of Man Fontana 1965

On The Sport

Tom Scott Burns and Martin Rigg — Round About the N. Y. Moors Rigg 1988

M. Hartley and J. Ingilby — Life in the Moorlands of N.E. Yorks Dent 1972

Brian Martin — Glorious Grouse David Charles 1990

Brian Martin — Tales of Old Gamekeepers David Charles 1989

Colin L. McKelvie — The Book of Woodcock Swan Hall 1986

Joseph Nickerson — Shooting Man's Creed Sidgewick & Jackson '89

John Welcolme & Rupert Collans — Snaffles (Life of Charles Johnson Payne 1884 - 1967) Stanley Paul 1987

BIBLIOGRAPHY II
Press Cuttings and Journals

The Field

Richard S. Sharpe Faith with the Fox Hunt p.68 Sept 1990 Edward Cyboult Off and Away p.66 Aug. 1990

The Earl Peel Moors Wake Up p.69 Aug. 1990

Jack Hargreaves Stubble Shoots p.71 Aug. 1990

Wilson Stephens Eyes Open p.73 Aug. 1990

Wilson Stephens Summing Up (The Shooting Code) p.82 (Special Summer issue 1990)

Michael Wigan Red Grouse far from an Endangered Speciesp88

Francis Fulford Who Shall Farm? p.82 July 1990

Gordon Brook-Shepherd Heather Legs p.104 June 1990 Pat Robins Low Pheasants p.94 May 1990

Nicholas Budgen M.P. Hunting's Health (EEC & Hunting) p.86 April 1990

Oscar Colburn Set -Aside Folly p.68 March 1990

David Sinclair Straight Thinking (on conservation) p.74 March 1990

Wilson Stephens Shooting Code p.86 March 1990

Gordon Brook-Shepherd Article on Europeans who shoot in U.K.) Jan

Francis Fulford Arcitle on Price of Pheasants) '90
Collapses)

Wilson Stephens Shooting's Future p.79 Christmas 1989

Gordon Brook-Shepherd Europe's Interference p.83 " "

Bertram Sample How the Land Lies p. 87 " "

" " Shooting Code p. 90 Nov. 1989

" " On Small Farms p.104 " "

" " Our Lost Stubbles p. 92 Oct. 1989

Wilson Stephens <u>Duck for Choice</u> p. 76 Sept.1989
2 Articles on Grouse shooting pp 74 & 76 Aug 1989
3 Articles on Foul Shooting pp 104 - 105 May 1989
Various articles on Bogus shoots pp 78 - 81 March 1989

Wilson Stephens <u>Killing Ground Shoot Threat to Sport</u>* p.52 June 1989

*The start of the series in the Field that led towards a Shooting Code and a review of shooting practice.

<u>The Times</u>
Leader <u>Country Matters</u> p.9 28.8.90
Simon Barnes <u>12th of Never on the Moors?</u> 11.8.89
Shirley Lancaster <u>Searching for Ourselves</u>
John Habgood <u>The Good, The Bad, and The Individual</u> 27.2.89
George Hill <u>Newcomers take exception to the realities of rural life</u> 7.4.90 p.6
Francesca Greenoak
<u>By Royal Design</u> 30.12.89
On Karl Marx Brian Griffiths
<u>How Rich Men Can Enter the Kingdom of Heaven</u> 2/6/88
Jack Straw <u>The Briton Who Put Workers in the Boardroom</u> (on Field Marshall Lord Robertson)
<u>Foundations of Peace</u> 21.12.1940
<u>The Guardian</u>
M. Cocker <u>European Bird Shooting and the Threat to Conservation</u> 25.7.89
F. Keating <u>The Hunt Protestors</u> P.M. 27.12.88

<u>The Independent</u>
As per ref. in text 10.3.89

Max Hastings The Listener 27.10.88
" " Country Life 02.02.89
" " Review 04.05.89

BIBLIOGRAPHY III

Miscellaneous Pamphlets & Periodicals

Game as a Farm Crop
Stoneleigh, Arthur Rank Centre Nov. 1989

Andrew Patterson 150 Years of British Farming B.F.F. 1989

British Field Sports Society
The Code of Good Shooting Practice
59 Kennington Road, London SE17PL

The Game Conservancy Trust
Game 2000 Fordingbridge, Hants, SP6 1EF

The Game Conservancy
Game and Shooting Crops : 2 1979
Wildfowl Management : 3 1969
Partridge Rearing : 4
Pheasant & Partridge Eggs : 5 1978
Disease of Gamebirds & Wildfowl : 6 1981
Pheasant Rearing & Releasing : 8 1983
Game in Winter : 14 1966
Forestry & Pheasants : 15 1967
Red Legged Partridges : 18 1983
Hatching Gamebirds : 11
Enemies of Game : 16
Grey Squirrels : 19

Hill & Robertson The Pheasant Ecology, Conservation and Management London/Blackwell 1986

MIA Woodburn The Pheasant Field Studies and Radio-tagging report

Industrial Christian Fellowships Quarterly
June 1990 Articles on wealth creation and industry, particularly A Bias Against Business Lord Caldecote, also in The Times 12 - 15.3.90
I.C.F. Secretary 16 Bank Hart Road, Oprington, BR6 OQD

Other Sources of Information
Learning from the Land
B.F.F. 1989 Published by. R.A.S.E.,
Nat. Agric. Centre, Stoneleigh, Kenilworth, Warwicks. CV8 2LZ
From the Farm to the Brewery and Back Again
The Brewers Society, 42 Portman Square, London W1H OBB
City Farmer
Nat. Fed. of City Farms,
The Old Vicarage, 66 Fraser Street, Windmill Hill, Bristol, BS3 4LY
The Farmer's Weekly
Carew House, Wallington, Surrey, SM6 0DX
Farming News
ACRE (Asspc. of Community Councils for Rural England)
Stable Yard, Fairford Park, Glos. GL7 4JQ
N.F.U. Leaflets and Publications
Rural Development Commission
i.e. Promoting Jobs and Communities in Rural England
141 Castle Street, Salisbury, Wilts.
Festival of Food and Farming 1989 (B.F.F. 1989)
The Christian Rural Trust, Dovedale House, Ilam, Derbs.
The Arthur Rank Centre) Stoneleigh, Kenilworth
Royal Agricultural Society of England) Warwicks CV8 2LZ
Min. of Agric. & Fisheries & Food London & Local
World Wildlife Fund etc.
Preface to Country Services Booklet: Sponsored by R.A.S.E. 1989
Church Services for the Farming Year for Town & Country Arthur Rank Centre, Stoneleigh

BBC 2 Thursday, 24.10.96 Programme on Hunting
"Nature Special : The Twenty - first Century Fox."

POSTSCRIPT

As to killing, the fundamentalists do get carried away, but any form of shooting is based on the age old practice of man hunting for his food as humanely and successfully as possible. Bonhoeffer agonised over killing Hitler, as some suggest today that Saddam Hussein should be too, but to remove a bloodthirsty tyrant is not in the same league as providing food, sport, enjoyment, income and indulging a few earthy instincts in their proper surroundings.

Another consideration is ownership and property and land being a vehicle of personal expression just as shooting is an expression of the personality. Here, perhaps, the Church of England is somewhat ambivalent about those who own estates, yet depends on them to fund or maintain its churches. Having had a shot gun in my hands since the age of 11 and at times having earned my keep beating, loading or helping with shoots the criticism of such sport goes deep with me. Now it is part of my parish life and its livelihood. I therefore humbly seek to explore it from a theological perspective, because there are more arguments to be found in its favour, while what there is to condemn would be condemned anyway as greed and lack of consideration. There is now a danger that the latest war cry of the Church of England is "green" based* and biased against what landowners do on their land. Here again I would hope to mitigate some of the unjust criticism from a theological point of view and encourage my own parishioners, if no one else, to reflect on their activities from a wider perspective.

* *Since printing see article "The Times" 15.9 90 by Clifford Longley and the report Faith in the Countryside September 1990 Churchman Publishing, Worthing.*

THE LAST COUNT

Shooting is classified as a sport but the real sport must be the grouse moor. Grouse shooting is not a commercial venture; even though income in Northumberland in '95 reached £100 per brace rent, it must be understood that profits will be more than consumed during lean years. The satisfaction lies in the conservation of wild species, maintaining a way of life for a community in certain areas, and the pleasure of sporting days with friends. I am reminded of one Lord Feversham in Edwardian times who one year on finding the bag was 999 for the day walked off from the butts until he had shot another to make 500 brace! In those days transport was on foot and with ponies so it was a long physical day for the beaters. Another season there was a dearth of grouse on the 12th August and as few the following day so the guns were packed up and he announced it was the end of the season. The same approach needs to continue without being dictated by commercial pressure.

Pheasant shooting will always be commercially viable but we must not allow it to be so at the cost to the bird in terms of how we value a pheasant and God's creation. If you cannot remember what you shot, perhaps you should not have shot so many and fewer birds could have been put down. It does approach poultry farming proportions. Because birds have not often been reared under a hen, the next Spring they do not know what to do, so wild stocks do not increase.

Partridges provide good sport but are difficult to rear artificially. There has certainly been malpractice in letting them out of crates and flushing them over guns in a valley below. Many people hope that set-aside would improve their chances but unless there is insect lift in the headlands and on the stubble, they will not stay for that is their preferred feed. Too much spraying still destroys their habitat.

Finally my heartfelt thanks to my sponsor for printing these thoughts and findings, may he enjoy many shooting days to come.

Toddy Hoare, Oct. '96